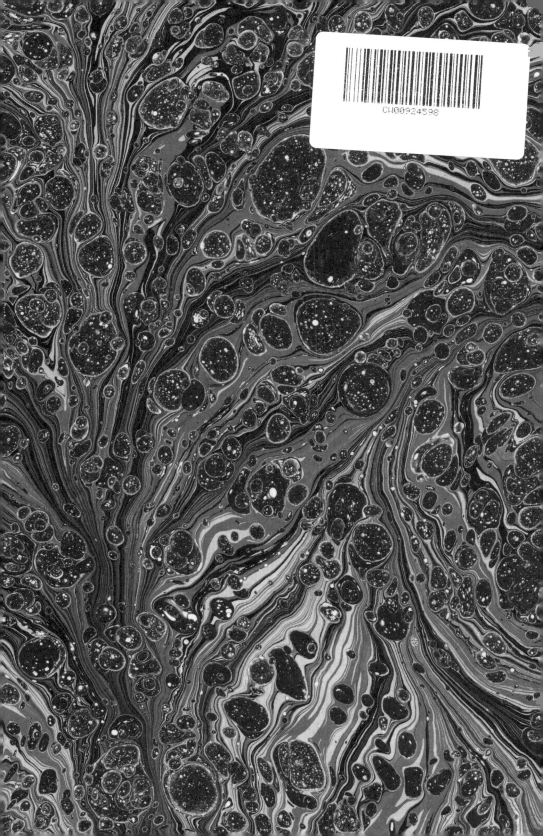

German Combat Divers in World War II

German Combat Divers
in World War II

Michael Jung
Translated from the German by David Johnston

Schiffer Military History
Atglen, PA

Book design by Robert Biondi.

Copyright © 2008 by Schiffer Publishing Ltd..
Library of Congress Catalog Number: 2008924542.

This book oroginally published under the title,
Sabotage unter Wasser: Die deutschen Kampfschwimmer im Zweiten Weltkrieg,
by Verlag E.S. Mittler & Sohn GmbH.

Printed in China.
ISBN: 978-0-7643-3092-6

We are always looking for people to write books on new and related subjects. If you have an idea for a book, please contact us at the address below.

Published by Schiffer Publishing Ltd.
4880 Lower Valley Road
Atglen, PA 19310
Phone: (610) 593-1777
FAX: (610) 593-2002
E-mail: Info@schifferbooks.com.
Visit our web site at: www.schifferbooks.com
Please write for a free catalog.
This book may be purchased from the publisher.
Please include $5.00 postage.
Try your bookstore first.

In Europe, Schiffer books are distributed by:
Bushwood Books
6 Marksbury Ave.
Kew Gardens, Surrey TW9 4JF
England
Phone: 44 (0)20 8392-8585
FAX: 44 (0)20 8392-9876
E-mail: info@bushwoodbooks.co.uk
www.bushwoodbooks.co.uk
Free postage in the UK. Europe: air mail at cost.
Try your bookstore first.

FOREWORD

"Here I would like to refute the commonly-held view
that these lone warriors of the Kriegsmarine
were men who had more or less finished with life.
It was thanks to our thorough and varied training
that casualties were very low.
This gratitude belongs to the former partner of deep sea researcher Hans Hass,
our instructor Leutnant Alfred von Wurzian."

Dr. Alfred Keller
Former leader of Combat Diver Group East[1]

"Sea commandos" – that is what the first combat divers of the German armed services called themselves. Established under the umbrella of the military secret service in 1943 as its "Sea Commando Battalion *Brandenburg*", in 1944 it was one of the most important cells of the navy's small battle force. Its field of operations was the reconnoitering and disabling of enemy ships and port installations as well as the destruction of bridges and locks in inland waterways to restrict or completely paralyze the enemy's advance or mobility. It also conducted various subversive commando and sabotage actions in enemy territory.

Until now almost nothing has been known about them, for all official documents on the subject were destroyed immediately before or after the war. Another reason why research into this special field has been so difficult is that most of the surviving veterans still feel bound by their oath of secrecy.

During years of research I have attempted to uncover the facts about the German combat divers of the Second World War in a scientific manner using established sources. In doing so I have been able to correct or add to the often one-sided and incomplete descriptions found in numerous publications. As well, in the process I have succeeded in uncovering the until now completely unknown story of the creation of the "Sea Commando Battalion Brandenburg" and the navy's Combat Diver Training Detachment 700 which emerged from it, as well as the history of the SS combat divers of the Reich Central Security Office's Dept. VI-S.

The memoirs of leading personalities, which became available after their deaths, are made public here for the first time. They offer an inside view of the force and finally show the true reasons behind the split between the navy and the SS in autumn 1944 – a significant event not only for naval historians.

Of central importance in my work were the handwritten and tape-recorded memories of Alfred von Wurzian, who was the driving force behind the formation of the first German combat diver unit under the umbrella of the military secret service, and who committed himself to it with great energy and personal dedication. Some of his autobiographical notes have survived and they served as the most important source for the following documentation. Important information also came from the war diary of the former commander of this close-knit community, naval officer Dr. Armin Wandel, which is also systematically evaluated and made publicly accessible for the first time here.

The work before you was only made possible through the kind support and the willing provision of archival material by Horst Ackermann, Franz Graf von Czernin-Chudenitz, Maurizio Dal Largo, Peter Dick, Manfred Dörr, Luigi Ferraro, Prof. Dr. Hans Hass, the Hummel family, Michael Hocke, Konrad Knirim, Manfred Lau, Dr. Stephan Linck, Dr. Hartmut Nöldeke, Reinhard Penninger, Heinz-Werner Sondermann, the Wurzian family, the staff of the Federal Archives in Berlin and Freiburg, in the Schleswig State Archive, and former members of LK 700, the small battle force and the *Abwehr* whose wish it was to remain anonymous.

Michael Jung
Merzig-Weiler, January 2004

CONTENTS

CHAPTER ONE

MILITARY DIVING
IN EARLIER TIMES

It is difficult to say with certainty which nation had the first underwater fighters. Many historical accounts are greatly exaggerated or simply invented. It does seem, however, that divers were employed frequently and for warlike purposes in antiquity. Warlords eager for booty recognized the great advantages a diver offered them in carrying out special tasks: his invisibility and ability to achieve surprise.

The first mention of the military use of divers appears in the chronicles of the Greek historian Herodotus ca. 450 BC. While in the service of the Persian king Xerxes, Skyllias of Skione near Alphetae retrieved goods from ships on the bottom of the sea and was richly rewarded with part of the proceeds. But Skyllias was secretly working for the enemy and during a storm cut the anchor lines of Persian ships near Pelion. Several of the ships thus set adrift were smashed on the rocks of Cape Artemision and sank. This enabled the Greeks to emerge victorious.

Almost all ancient navies employed working divers who made ship repairs or scouted channels and harbors during maritime sieges. They also cleared underwater obstacles. An example of this is provided by the Athenian siege of Syracuse during the Peloponnesian War. Syracuse, the most powerful city on the east coast of Sicily, was under siege by Athenian forces. In the harbor were many commercial vessels, which the Athenians had their eye on. The Syracusians, however, had realized that their merchant fleet was more important than their houses and did everything they could to prevent them from falling into enemy hands. Pilings were driven into the sea bed. Their tips were supposed to pierce the hulls of enemy ships, but divers sawed off these wooden pilings under water. During the battle divers were also used to bore holes in the hulls of enemy ships.

The chronicler of the Peloponnesian War, Thucydides – squadron commander, strategist and historian – provided a detailed description of the destruction of Syracuse's defensive installations by divers ca. 414 BC. Divers also saw action off Orikon. The inhabitants had sunk ships weighed down with stones in the harbor to block the entrance. Pompeius subsequently used divers to remove the stones and refloat the ships, which were then removed, reopening the port.

The historian Pausanias makes reference to Alexander the Great's use of ships to deliver siege engines to Tyros (322 BC), located in what is now Lebanon. Enemy divers cut the anchor lines, however, and foiled the attack. Concerning the three-year siege of Byzantium by the Romans under Emperor Severus, it was reported that one day the besiegers' ships began moving slowly toward the harbor. Neither sails nor oars were used: Byzantian divers had cut the anchor ropes and installed tow ropes in their place.

What sort of equipment did these early divers use? Surely they had few other swimming aids apart from air-filled goatskins or reed mats, which enabled them to cover long distances while conserving their strength. One can surmise that they used breathing aids like snorkels, but unfortunately we do not know this for certain.

The military use of divers eventually became so important that defensive measures were devised. Usually these consisted of nets to which warning devices, like bells, were attached, but cutters were also added at a later date. Also used were rotating beams fitted with blades, intended to injure enemy divers. As early as the 2nd Century BC the Romans replaced all anchor lines with iron chains and had their own harpoon-armed divers guard their ships in unsafe waters.

Divers were also often used to gather intelligence, to sneak into then enemy camp, to transport food and other tasks. For example, when the Athenians were laying siege to the Lacedaemonians in the port of Messina, swimmers brought news and food through enemy lines. The same was reported from the Roman encirclement of the city of Numantia in Castile. As swimmers were smuggling food across the Duero River, Scipio had it barricaded with beams on which swords and spears had been mounted. The beams were anchored to the shore and spun with the current.

The use of diving as a source of revenue led to the formation of the first commercial diving company in Rome in the 2nd Century BC. Its name was *Urinatore*. It was a guild, combining divers and fishermen, governed by its own by-laws and headed by a respected patron. It went into action after various accidents on the Tiber and at sea, recovering articles from the bottom for a fee. These divers also repaired ships and took part in military actions for pay. The *Urinatores* formed a military component which was entrusted with special missions and surprise raids. They brought food into cities under siege, towing goatskin bags filled with grain behind them, and delivered news and orders which were scratched into lead plates on bracelets. Finally they also destroyed enemy defensive installations.

Diving for military purposes is present from antiquity through the Middle Ages and in all societies. In the Middle Ages, for example, knightly training included physical fitness along with training in courtly behavior and battle techniques. Diving was widely practiced. The importance of diving at that time is probably best reflected in the fact that it was one of the "seven physical skills of the knight".

In 1500 Leonardo da Vinci described a special tool for the destruction of ships by divers. It was a device for boring into ships. The diver was supposed to drill a hole into the wooden hull of the ship, if possible at the end of a plank. Then he placed a clamping claw over the small hole. Into the hole he placed a screw with a small lever device on its head which, when tensioned, spread and held the device firmly on the plank. The diver then turned the claw and pulled the plank away from the hull until water was able to enter the ship. His work done, the diver then departed. The crew was unable to loosen or remove the clamping claw from the inside.

Swimming with the aid of an air-filled bladder, Paolo di Cassia of Calabria stole up to the Turkish fleet off the Iles du Levant and set it afire with gunpowder.

Although combat divers frequently played important roles in war, there is almost nothing written about them after the siege of Malta by the Turks in 1565. The Vizier Mustafa, who was laying siege to Malta, employed his axe-armed swimming brigade to destroy a defensive palisade. The Turks entered the water, but they were attacked by Maltese swimmers before they could reach the installation. A frightful battle in the water ensued, from which the Maltese emerged victorious.

The importance of combat swimmers seems to have diminished after this event, and the last account we find of them comes from Louis XIV's navy. The divers, called *Mourgons*, were from the officer ranks, however they had no important military function and were only used to inspect and repair the hulls of ships.

The first German concepts for combat divers can be traced back to the middle of the 18th Century. They were the brainchild of Count Wilhelm von Schaumburg-Lippe, one of the most important military reformers of the German enlightenment. Count Wilhelm was the first to institute compulsory military service because, as he said, "no one defends a land with more determination than one who lives there." The count himself invented a breech-loading gun and had the maritime fortress of Wilhelmstein built on a manmade island in Steinhuder Lake near Bückeburg. It was at his military academy that the famous Gerhard Johann David von Scharnhorst learned the skills he would later put to use in the Prussian Army.

The count had many ideas about how to improve the defensive readiness and military power of his state, in particular the fortress at Wilhelmstein. His inventions included folding boats and swimming aids for horses, and he considered the use of armed swimmers in Steinhuder Lake: "In 1758 I conducted a test in assisting horses to swim through the use of leather-covered ox bladders slung over the breast and shoulders on both sides. This invention made it possible for a rider to safely cover a very great distance in the water. The invention might possibly be useful in a blockade, especially when returning riders cannot be picked up by ships in time. It would be a good idea to have some young people practice swimming and diving. They could be very useful in many circumstances."[2]

Unfortunately it is not known if Count Wilhelm actually trained and used armed swimmers. But we do know with certainty about the German use of armed swimmers in the First World War, albeit on a small scale: in 1915 an experimental company of the Potsdam Guards Battalion tested a swimming platoon. Among their equipment was a carrying rack with pouches for explosive charges. The unit carried out its first and probably only operation on the night of 17 August 1915. Five pioneers of the 2nd Reserve Pioneer Company, formed by the Stettin Pioneer Battalion No. 2, sank a Russian steamer lying off the Niemen fortress of Kovno. Although the attack was successful, no more missions were conducted. Until 1944 the German Navy had only working divers with no combat role. The possible use

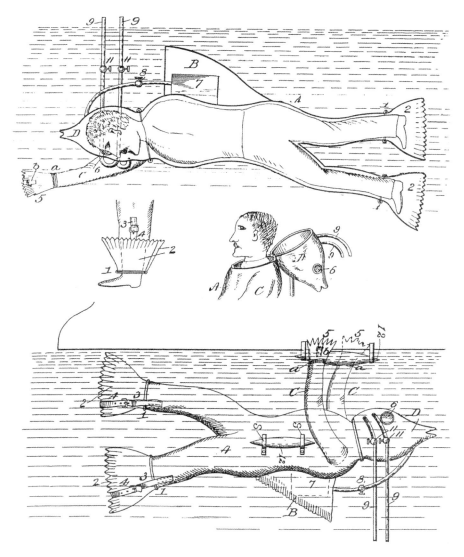

A curious idea for equipping a combat diver: patented in 1898, this invention by the American James J. Devine consisted of a fish-like diving suit with two fixed snorkel tubes in the area of the head. To dive, the wearer closed both tubes and opened the valve of the pressurized air tank in the dorsal fin. On the suit were fittings for mines, which the diver was supposed to attach to the bilge keels of enemy ships.

of divers for offensive purposes was not rediscovered in Germany until near the end of the Second World War, when they were employed on a larger scale.

CHAPTER TWO

EARLY HISTORY

The story of the German combat diver force began in mid-July 1942 in Piraeus Harbor and the name of its founder was Alfred von Wurzian.[3] The Austrian was then a member of marine researcher Hans Hass' Aegean expedition. Wurzian had known Hass since autumn 1937 and through him had become an experienced diver and skilled underwater cameraman. Wurzian was studying law at the University of Vienna and had just completed a stint as a "one-year volunteer" with an Austrian mountain artillery unit.

A vacation trip to the south of France in July 1937 had led to Hans Hass's first encounter with the undersea world. Fascinated by the underwater hunt, from then on Hass was an avid spearfisherman. Very soon, however, his investigative spirit was awakened: no longer did he just want to hunt fish like wild game, instead he yearned to learn more about the unexpectedly varied marine-biological processes. After returning from southern France, therefore, Hass planned to begin zoological studies, but his father, a well-known and influential lawyer in Vienna, urged him to study law so that he might one day take over his thriving practice. And so Hass and Wurzian met as students in the University of Vienna's law faculty, and as both were members of the academic sports association in Vienna, they shared many interests.

In addition to a passion for research, adventurer's blood flowed in the veins of Hans Hass, and thus it was that he carried out his first expedition in 1938. On that occasion several comrades from the university in Vienna accompanied him to Yugoslavia. In addition to underwater fishing with spear and goggles, Hass took his first underwater photographs with a homemade waterproof camera. Swim fins were also used on this expedition. They offered an underwater photographer the inestimable advantage of being able to swim with the legs alone, leaving the hands free to operate the camera.

Hass also gathered his first experience with breathing apparatuses on this expedition: based on the work of the American naturalist William Beebe, he had built his own open diving helmet with air pump. Hass soon recognized the disadvantages of the open helmet for underwater research: the air bubbles noisily exiting the rim of the helmet and the air hose disturbed the nearby fish and chased them away. There was thus little opportunity to observe or photograph them. As well, the diving helmet tied him to the bottom and limited his movements to walking. He was restricted to a small circle of sea bottom around the boat, and he could not go where the bottom was uneven. The open diving helmet's only advantage was that it allowed him to stay longer under water.

On Hass' next expedition in 1939 he was again forced to retain the unsatisfactory open diving helmet. This trip took him and his two friends Alfred von Wurzian and Jörg Böhler to Curacao and Bonaire in the Caribbean. There the three friends experienced the excitement of underwater fishing but also the dangers of equipment diving: while diving off the coast of Bonaire Wurzian had a decompression accident and was fortunate to escape serious injury.

The sudden outbreak of the Second World War obliged the three men to remain in Curacao longer than anticipated, and they were forced to return to Vienna by way of the USA, China and Russia. The expedition and trip home lasted a total of 18 months – from July 1939 to September 1940. In addition to much new experience, Hass returned from the expedition with film for a short feature titled "Stalk Under Water". In 1942 it was shown in theaters as an UFA short before the newsreels.

As some additional filming in the Adriatic was required for the film and Wurzian wanted to complete his law studies, he was initially exempted from military service. Not until early 1942 did he enter the military, and on 20 March he was attached to the 3rd Company of the102nd Light Artillery Replacement Battalion (mot.) in Olmütz, Moravia as an *Unteroffizier* (reserve officer candidate). His marked sense of justice and fearlessness even in the presence of superior ranks resulted in six weeks in a punishment company and the loss of his officer candidacy: Wurzian had opposed the harassment of members of his battalion by superiors and exposed several officers. Wurzian's service in the *Wehrmacht* did not last very long, however, for he was also to take part in Hans Hass' next underwater expedition, planned for the summer of 1942.

After returning from the Caribbean, Hans Hass had finally abandoned his law studies, and against his father's wishes he began studying zoology. He dreamed of other expeditions to the coral seas of the southern hemisphere, where he could see and study many unknown plants and animals.

Beginning in 1941 Hass wrote books and magazine articles and gave countless speeches to raise money. He dreamed of having his own research ship and helping in the spread of new research methods. At the same time, he wanted to show that sharks were not the cold-blooded monsters they were often portrayed as, and that they did not bar the way to the deeps for the researcher. Hass planned an additional expedition for the summer of 1942, but because of the war it would have to take place in the Mediterranean, not the tropical seas. He wanted to use the expedition to demonstrate for the first time the advantage of the great freedom of movement bestowed by the combination of swim fins and autonomous diving equipment.

To Hass an oxygen circulation system seemed best suited. It worked on the principle of the closed breathing system with fresh oxygen feed and the absorption of exhaled carbon dioxide by breathing lime (barium or soda lime). The system was originally devised to save trapped submarine crews and miners. Based on a design by the Englishmen Henry Fleuss and Robert David, it was an extremely simple device: the diver breathed through a mouthpiece which was connected by a rubber hose to a bag. This soft bag was inflated by exhalation and deflated by inhalation, forcing the air to pass through a filter containing breathing lime, which absorbed carbon dioxide. A small bottle with highly compressed oxygen was attached to the bag. On the first devices the valve on the bottle had to be operated by hand. The diver could thus maintain the desired percentage of oxygen in the breathing air in the bag and compensate for the increased pressure when diving. The circulatory system was equipped with a safety valve to allow excess pressure to be released during ascent.

In early 1941 Hass had visited Dräger, the leading manufacturer of diving equipment in Germany, in Lübeck. Already in 1928 Dräger had designed the so-called "counter lung", a submarine rescue device consisting of a ring-shaped air bag worn around the neck. This air bag was supposed to assist in walking upright on the sea bottom and provide its wearer with a safe means of reaching the surface when used as a rescue device.

Dräger's oxygen circulation system was small, light and easy to use. Attached to the belt was a 0.6-liter oxygen bottle whose contents were under 200 bar of pressure. According to the makers, a diver could conduct moderately strenuous work at a depth of ten to fifteen minutes for up to one hour. On the bottle was an automatic metering valve, and a constant quantity of pure oxygen flowed through a narrow tube into the breathing bag. The diver breathed from this bag by means of a flexible hose with mouthpiece, and a second hose transferred the breathing air back into the bag, passing through a lime filter in the process. The bag could be opened and resealed, so that fresh lime could be added before each dive.

Though simple in design, the first oxygen circulation devices were by their nature both difficult and dangerous to use: first there was the danger of oxygen shortage if the device's breathing bag and the diver's lungs were not emptied before diving. If the breathing bag received atmospheric air containing a high percentage of nitrogen and the air in the lungs with its high percentage of nitrogen was also breathed into the bag, after some time the breathing bag received only nitrogen, which was inhaled.

Prior to diving, therefore, all normal air had to be removed from the lungs and the diving equipment. The lime filter did not affect the nitrogen content of about 78% of breathing air, as it only absorbed carbon dioxide. If the oxygen content in the gas mixture dropped after several breaths, this was not noticed as missing volume because of the quantity of nitrogen remaining in the air bag. After a certain period of time the diver was breathing only nitrogen. Before diving, therefore, the breathing bag had to contain only oxygen, and a special breathing technique – "rinsing" several times before diving – was used to remove as much nitrogen from the lungs and air bag as possible.

Another problem arose if the breathing lime became wet, for this reduced its effectiveness. This happened, for example, if the mouthpiece was removed without closing the blocking valve, allowing water to reach the lime. Water combined with the lime to form corrosive caustic soda. Improper filling of the breathing lime could lead either to inadequate carbon dioxide absorption or to excessive breathing resistance. As well, when combined with grease, oxygen becomes flammable and explosive – therefore no components that might come into contact with the oxygen could be greased.

Together with Senior Engineer Hermann Stelzner, Dräger's technical director, Hass modified the "counter-lung" to meet his requirements. There followed a number of patented improvements which, through changes to the breathing bag and in combination with fins, turned the counter-lung into a swim-diving device. The air bag was moved to the back for improved center of gravity, and the use of a diving mask which covered both the eyes and mouth was a decisive improvement. A nose clamp was used to equalize pressure during deep dives. The use of swim fins turned the autonomous oxygen circulation device into a swim-diving device. From a technical point of view the swim-diving device exhibited only minor changes, but it differed fundamentally from earlier devices in the way it was used: instead of walking upright on the sea bottom – the position in which the water offered the most resistance – the swim-diving device made possible the only physically-correct method of propulsion, the one used by all sea mammals, namely with the head forward and fins on the rear extremities.

Alfred von Wurzian, during the Aegean expedition in 1942.

Hass was able to lead an expedition into the Aegean in 1942. This historical event was documented in his movie "Men among Sharks". In the film Hass described his feelings during his first dive: "I immediately allowed myself to sink to a depth of 10 meters. It was a wonderful feeling to be able to spend time under water with no breathing difficulties and complete freedom of movement. I had truly become an amphibious creature and could swim with the fish!"

Hass risked his life to determine the performance limits of the device, and two potentially serious accidents demonstrated the high risks associated with the oxygen circulation system. The main problem resulted from the fact that oxygen became poisonous at a pressure of 1.6 bar, or from a depth of about 6 meters. Even at that comparatively shallow depth, neurological symptoms could develop within minutes. The typical symptoms of oxygen poisoning were nausea, dizziness, blurred vision, feelings of anxiety, hearing loss and cramps. The cramps posed the most serious threat, as they also appeared in the face and could result in the loss of the mouthpiece. Unable to replace it, the diver drowned. It was impossible to clearly determine the sequence, warning signs and intensity of the individual symptoms. In its insidious nature lay oxygen poisoning's greatest danger. As well, an immediate reduction in depth did not always result in the immediate disappearance of the symptoms. All of this was not well known at that time, for according to the manufacturer it was possible to dive to 20 meters with the equipment.

Hass continued using the circulation system on his expedition in spite of the risks and dangers. It functioned almost silently, the only sound being the soft clicking of the valves in the two breathing hoses. Another advantage was that it was compact and easy to use and could almost fit in a briefcase. Pure oxygen was available in almost every port in the world, as it was used for welding. And so each expedition only had to take along the necessary breathing lime, about 80 kilograms for 100 hours of diving.

Another factor in favor of the circulation device was its ability to use a helium-oxygen mixture instead of pure oxygen. Given the right mixture, the depth limit could theoretically be extended to 250 meters. In 1941, however, the only source of sufficient quantities of helium was the USA. The process of producing helium from air, as was practiced in Germany at that time, was much too expensive and time-consuming.[4]

CHAPTER THREE

FROM UNDERWATER FILMMAKER TO SABOTAGE SPECIALIST

While Hass was thinking about the new possibilities which the diving equipment offered for marine research, his fellow expedition member Alfred von Wurzian came up with the idea of employing it for military purposes. As it produced no air bubbles on the surface to betray the diver's position, to Wurzian it seemed eminently suitable for combat divers, who job it was to secretly place charges on enemy vessels and carry out other tasks under water.

Wurzian knew of possible uses for the new equipment from Japanese experience: during the First World War they had employed swimmers in the capture of Tsingtao. With no kind of mechanical aid, using only their physical strength, armed swimmers swam to shore and joined the fighting. Another example was more recent: in December 1941 the English and Canadian defenders of Hong Kong had surrendered to the Japanese, beginning an occupation of the island that would last more than three years. After the surrender Japanese swimmer battalions had cleared the coastal minefields.

Alfred von Wurzian began working on a similar plan. As a member of the military and a lover of the sea, he thought that he might usefully combine the two. Wurzian's basic idea was to equip combat divers with the oxygen circulation system and swim fins. Submarines would drop them off near enemy harbors at night and they would then place explosive charges on enemy ships.

Hass had succeeded in interesting the navy and the Reich research council in his marine biological work and they gave their support to his Aegean expedition. Among the participants was Alfred von Wurzian, who had been placed on leave by the military. On 11 July 1942 the commanding admiral in the Aegean, *Vizeadmiral* Erich Förste, visited the men before the departure of the expedition. Wurzian used the opportunity to propose his combat diver idea and demonstrate the silent diving equipment at the mole in Piraeus. As there was only one set of diving gear available at that moment and Hans Hass had planned a dive to investigate the fauna in the harbor area that day anyway, Hass made the demonstration dive himself, while Wurzian stayed on the shore with the admiral and the chief of staff, *Korvettenkapitän z.S.* Rothe-Roth. He explained the proceedings to the two officers and promoted his idea.

The dive was supposed to last ten minutes, but Hans Hass was so enthralled by the underwater world on the outer side of the mole that he completely forgot the time and the observers on the surface and stayed under for more than 45 minutes. When he finally surfaced, he found the two officers very angry that their departure had been delayed. At first their interest in the new diving equipment and Wurzian's combat diver idea appeared to have been extinguished, but the next day Förste gave a detailed report to his superiors in Naval Group Command South in Sofia as he was duty bound to do. The chief of staff there received the report on Hass and Wurzian's demonstration and studied it with great interest. His name was *Kapitän z.S.* Hellmuth Heye.

At almost the same time Heye, whose post was also responsible for the Admiral in command of the Black Sea, witnessed firsthand the successful use of the Italian naval unit *"Decima Mas"* in the siege of the naval fortress of Sevastopol.[5] Heye had high regard for the Italian special unit's striking power and usefulness. He recognized the value that a similar special unit would have for the German side and became the advocate and pioneer for this type of special unit. Earlier, in June 1941, Heye had formed and led the "Naval Operations Detachment Black Sea" – the first special unit of its kind in the German navy. Three years later it would be integrated into the small battle force.

Heye later explained why it took so long for a German small battle unit on the Italian model to be formed within the navy: "The reasons for German reservations about small unit warfare were probably of a psychological nature. Belief in the effectiveness of large numbers and 'mass' and the neglect of individuality seems to me to have been a characteristic of our times. Such attitudes are, however, closely associated with any type of totalitarian system and under an Adolf Hitler they of course extended to military questions. Thus it was that the problem of the lone fighter and the small battle unit was not addressed until the zenith of military success and thus the superiority of numbers was already in decline."[6]

After returning from the Aegean in November 1942, Wurzian initially returned to the normal military routine of an NCO and instructor in his unit, the 102nd

Artillery Replacement Battalion (mot.) in Olmütz. He had not abandoned his idea of a military use for diving, as the impressions formed on the recently completed expedition had been too strong: "Whether diving to the wrecks off the port of Piraeus or swimming around Piraeus harbor in the evening twilight, the idea of using divers in a military role never left me. And what possibilities it offered – to approach an enemy vessel or enter a harbor unseen."[7] And again: "1942 was a year in which everyone was filled with courage and activity. The idea of a combat diver never left me. That is what I called the swimmer. Many nights I could not sleep, a new idea came to me every minute, each more daring than the last."[8]

In Olmütz Wurzian made every effort to promote his idea, and the battalion medical officer proved very interested. He subsequently arranged a meeting with the commanding officer of the artillery unit, and Wurzian knew how to exploit the opportunity. He described his idea to the *Oberst* in detail: "The combat diver swims in the fully prone position, not allowing any part of his body to break the surface of the water, wearing swim fins on his feet. If the water is cold he wears a suit of dark canvas. While not waterproof, the suit does keep the current off the body. While swimming, the water warmed by the body remains inside the suit and cools only very slowly.[9] The breathing equipment is worn on the chest. At 100 to 200 meters from the target the mouthpiece is placed in the mouth and the diver then swims to the target beneath the surface of the water. On reaching the ship's hull he places the explosive charge. The charge is circular in shape and is equipped with a magnet around its circumference. The magnet is powerful enough to secure the charge to the hull even when the vessel is in motion. The fuse is not inserted until just before the diver enters the water. This means that the charge is transported on land without a fuse, the fusing mechanism remaining separate from the charge. Everything must be assembled before the mission. It is possible, however, to delay detonation for up to 24 hours using a clockwork mechanism. This is designed to give the diver sufficient time to swim away from the exploding bomb. While observing dynamite fisherman in the Aegean, I have seen exploding charges cause burst eardrums at a distance of approximately 500 meters. At a distance of 200 meters exploding bombs even crushed thoraxes."[10]

Wurzian gave such an impassioned and convincing description of the military potential of submerged swimming that his commanding officer granted him three months special leave to present his idea directly to the authorities in Berlin. The day after his interview, with leave pass and ticket to Berlin in hand, Wurzian already felt himself one significant step closer to his goal. In fact, however, it was the beginning of a tiresome hurdle race for Wurzian.

Arriving in Berlin in mid-December 1942, the enthusiastic Wurzian first went to the navy, which was responsible for the Research, Invention and Patent Office

(FEP) in the Naval Weapons Central Office of the Navy High Command/Naval Equipment. When Wurzian presented his ideas to the committee, its members merely shook their heads in disbelief: a lone man taking on heavily armored warships? A lone diver could only transport a small charge to the target, and that was supposed to sink a battleship? The navy committee, which was thinking in quite different dimensions and scales, thought Wurzian's ideas impracticable and actually laughed at him. "I was furious and left the room without saluting", Wurzian described his feelings.[11] He next turned to the army department responsible for combat engineers. It had on staff experts familiar with diving technology and had even used divers for various underwater tasks. This quickly proved to be a handicap, however, for they were so convinced of their own capabilities that they saw no reason to create a new formation with underwater fighters.

Wurzian's presentation in the operational headquarters of the SS was especially frustrating. The officer in charge of the "Weapons Inspectorate" department declared to him that there was no requirement for such lone warriors because final victory would soon be at hand. Wurzian was told that he should return to his unit immediately so that he could do his duty at the front.

During those weeks in early 1943 Wurzian lived in Berlin-Charlottenburg. He used his spare time to give presentations to authorities as a representative of Hans Hass, who was working on his doctorate. He also gave public lectures about the Aegean expedition as part of the "Strength through Joy" movement. From January to March 1943 Wurzian carried out a five-week speaking tour in cities in Saxony and Thuringia. Unlike his earlier presentations to the authorities, the speeches were a great success. On many days he gave two speeches and once in Weimar he spoke to an audience of 1,000.

It was not until the end of January 1943, after a meeting with *Oberst* Erwin Lahousen-Vivremont of the *OKW-Amt Ausland/Abwehr*, the military secret service, that further perspectives developed for Wurzian's ideas. Department II of the secret service – abbreviated "*Abwehr II*" – was commanded by *Admiral* Wilhelm Canaris and was responsible for sabotage, anti-sabotage and the preparation and execution of commando operations. One of the principal objectives of this central office for sabotage, which was initially responsible for all agencies conducting such operations at home and abroad during times of war and peace, was to locate, recruit and train men qualified to carry out these multifarious missions.

As all of these missions demanded trained soldiers and outstanding individual fighters, a secret "*Abwehr* private army" was created, which later became the *Brandenburg* Division. Its name derived from the site of its initial formation in the city of Brandenburg not far from Berlin. This first regular German commando unit was made up of specially qualified soldiers and excellently-trained individual fighters, the majority of whom volunteered for this special unit. Dubbed "*Brandenburgers*", these *Abwehr* soldiers saw action on every front in Europe as well as in Asia and Africa. Masters of camouflage and disguise, they slipped through the front lines in enemy uniforms, carried out daring assault and reconnaissance operations, and conducted risky actions together with foreign volunteers or rebellious colonial peoples. The unit operated under the strictest secrecy, consequently there are few official reports about its actions.

Oberst Lahousen was the first official to show any real interest in Alfred von Wurzian's ideas. Since the summer of 1942, Canaris and Walter Schellenberg, head of the foreign intelligence service in the SS Reich Central Security Office, had been aware of Italy's successful use of underwater sabotage units. Both had attended a meeting of the "Spain-Portugal War Organization" in Madrid, where they heard about successful attacks by Italian "*Gamma* swimmers" at Gibraltar, however no specifics had been given as to equipment or tactics.[12]

Thanks to Alfred von Wurzian, *Oberst* Lahousen now saw an opportunity for Germany to use this sabotage technology more efficiently than before. Lahousen introduced Wurzian to his organization's specialists in sabotage equipment and the director of *Abwehr II*'s Section T (Technology) in Berlin-Tegel, Senior Engineer Neumeyer. Neumeyer was a civilian employee of the *Abwehr* and his role was similar to that of the famous "Mr. Q" in the James Bond stories: in Tegel Neumeyer headed a secret research facility for the development of specialized equipment and devices of all kinds. This special laboratory was a miniature marvel of technology, inventive skill and resourcefulness. Explosives specialists, chemists, designers and fine mechanics worked round the clock devising new and better equipment for use in missions by the special forces.

Closely associated with the research and development laboratory was *Abwehr II*'s training school for sabotage tactics, located on a small, idyllic farm on Lake Quenz in Brandenburg. Its cover name was "Quenz Farm", and the facility was heavily guarded and sealed off from the outside world. There were living quarters, training buildings and firing ranges, while scattered about the farm were sections of wooden and iron bridges, lengths of railroad track and a series of other training objects. They were used to practice covert approach, the silent elimination of sentries and finally the correct placing of explosives. Located in an isolated old barn, an original part of the farm, was the so-called "Witch's Kitchen". There future special agents were shown how to make explosives and detonators using common materials. Hidden behind dense pine forests there was a small fishpond and extensive sand pits in which other realistic exercises were carried out.

Other subjects taught at Quenz Farm were foreign languages, the art of camouflage and disguise, the manufacturing of passes and documents, transmission of intelligence and the tactic of subversive warfare. In addition the soldiers learned to ride, fly, parachute jump, use radio equipment and handle enemy weapons.

Almost every *Abwehr* man and *Brandenburger* destined for special commandos passed through this "Combat and Intelligence School" and was trained in accordance with the classic rules of the intelligence service. Altogether, this agent school on Quenz Lake was fully capable of providing modern secret service training to agents and instructors, giving them a solid background in the technology and tactics of sabotage and the equipment they might be expected to use.

Neumeyer quickly recognized the value of Wurzian's expert knowledge in the field of diving, for Neumeyer had already amassed some personal experience in ship sabotage.[13] One member of Neumeyer's department was *Oberleutnant* Martiny, whose main responsibility was the development of new methods for sabotaging ships. This represented one of the most difficult fields for the *Abwehr*, for most experiments failed because of its inability to deliver the amount of explosives required to sink a freighter beneath the water unseen. Approaching the ships, which were heavily guarded during on- and off-loading, was difficult enough, but transporting the necessary explosive charges to a part of the ship that would result in its sinking was calculated to be next to impossible. The number of ships of both sides sunk by agent sabotage during the Second World War was comparatively small.

All that was left therefore was minor acts of sabotage, which now and then caused an unexplained fire on a ship, damage to its propulsion system or a mysterious explosion on an upper deck. Serious damage or the total loss of a ship could only be expected in rare cases where a relatively easy to smuggle detonator was successfully planted on explosives or ammunition already on board.

Abwehr II had already trained five specialists for marine sabotage, and they were earmarked for operations against ships in Spanish ports. They were to enter the water from the quay near the ships and place their explosive charges. The most successful *Abwehr* agent in this field was Friedrich Hummel, who operated in southern Spain, mainly in the port of Gibraltar. Once, operating from La Linea, Hummel succeeded in destroying a British patrol boat in the port of Gibraltar by detonating the mines on board the vessel. Such successes were quite rare, however.

Already in 1939, the *Abwehr* had been ordered to interdict Allied marine traffic in the Mediterranean and Black Seas through acts of sabotage. The bases from which these attempts were made were Greek, Bulgarian and Rumanian ports. In order to avoid difficulties with the still-neutral Balkan nations, the explosives had to be set off outside the three-mile limit. Translated into the language of sabotage technology, this necessitated the use of long-delay detonators and a thorough preliminary investigation of the freighters' stay in port and their sailing schedules. Unforeseen events, such as might happen anywhere at any time, obviously increased the difficulty of such sabotage attacks. On one occasion the *Abwehr* succeeded in placing explosives in barrels of jam which were to be loaded onto a British freighter in a Greek port. The explosives had been placed in the barrels while still in the hands of the shipping contractor in Belgrade. The time required to transport the barrels to the loading port had to be determined, as well as the freighter's scheduled sailing time and the amount of time required to clear the three-mile zone. Then a safety margin was added. The necessary long-delay detonators were procured in Switzerland. The explosion eventually took place on the high seas. Serious damage was done to the interior and superstructure of the ship, but this was not sufficient to cause it to sink.

A curious incident occurred during a similar operation in 1940: British freighters were using Bulgarian Black Sea ports to deliver supplies to the French Levant Army in Syria. The plan called for explosives to be smuggled aboard these ships during the loading of coal. The *Abwehr* laboratory in Tegel had prepared chunks of coal containing explosives which could be mixed with the ships' coal. The heat of combustion was supposed to set off the explosives and seriously damage the boiler.

The selected British vessel sailed into the port of Varna as anticipated, however the ship's captain unexpectedly refused to accept the coal, declaring it to be of poor quality. The freighter instead sailed back to another port. Then, to the *Abwehr*'s dismay, an Italian cargo ship which arrived shortly after the British vessel purchased the prepared coal. In order to save the boilers of the fellow Axis partner's ship, the *Abwehr* had no choice but to inform their colleagues of the Bulgarian secret service. Arrangements were made to quickly buy back the affected coal at an inflated price.

It made no difference what cargo was used to smuggle explosives and detonators aboard Allied ships – coal, ore, oranges. Only in the rarest of cases was this sufficient to result in sinking, and then only small vessels. At the *Abwehr* laboratory, therefore, Neumeyer began thinking about devices which would make it possible to launch remotely-controlled explosive-carrying boats and special torpedoes against ships in port from a motor- or sailboat.

For example, Neumeyer experimented with remotely-controlled torpedoes, which were to be launched from hidden bunkers along the length of the Atlantic Wall in the event of an Allied invasion. Two soldiers would guard each bunker, which would house 20 remotely-controlled torpedoes and underwater launch ramps. The torpedoes were launched with the push of a button and were subsequently guided by VHF radio. The torpedo ran just beneath the surface of the water. On its back was a tall spine, which stuck out of the water like a mast or the fin of a shark, revealing the torpedo's path to the controller on shore. Farther back there was a rearwards-facing electric lamp. The controller had to keep the lamp and the spine aligned, exactly like the sights of a rifle, in order to control direction. If the torpedo missed its target, it could be turned by radio control for another pass. The disadvantage of this was that the rear-facing light became visible to the target during the turn, alerting it to the threat of attack. In the spring of 1943 Wurzian personally took part in several test firings of remotely-guided torpedoes and was amazed by their accuracy.[14]

The technical problems had been solved, but development of a practical weapon did not take place. The reason for this was the lack of cooperation from the navy, which of course had much deeper technical experience with torpedoes. The reason behind this was undoubtedly *Abwehr* chief Canaris' poor relationship with Raeder, and things became even worse when he was succeeded by Dönitz. Canaris was not especially well regarded by the *Kriegsmarine*. The sole exception was the *Abwehr*'s observation post in Algericas, whose sole purpose was to monitor shipping movements in the Strait of Gibraltar for the navy. The conflicts between the *Abwehr* and the *Kriegsmarine* would later prove a major obstacle in the formation of the combat diver force.

Until the beginning of 1943, the *Abwehr*'s only way of striking enemy shipping was costly and only moderately successful sabotage strikes against ships in port or at the roadstead. Strict security measures in coastal waters prevented any such attacks on enemy warships, however. Considering the size of torpedo warhead required to sink a medium-size armored warship, it becomes obvious that no normal agent could convey such a quantity of explosives, in his rucksack so to speak, into the interior of a ship. All that was left was sabotage of the ship's machinery which, though possible, could only inflict limited damage. A requirement for this type of sabotage, and of course for attacks with explosives, was a sympathetic person within the ship's crew. At the end of 1942 *Feldmarschall* Wilhelm Keitel delivered an order to the *Abwehr* to carry out a "large-scale sabotage action" against the French fleet in Toulon to stop it from putting to sea. The order was an amateurish one, impossible to carry out with the existing means.

From February 1943 on, Wurzian regularly visited Neumeyer in Tegel, telling him of his technical knowledge and his ideas about underwater warfare. For Wurzian this was the beginning of a happy time, for because of his special leave "no one was responsible for me. I received my rations, my pay, and the name of my old artillery division was always entered in my paybook. But in reality I was all alone and independent in this highly-organized state."[15] During this time Wurzian learned about sabotage techniques and the associated equipment in the laboratory in Tegel and the combat school at Quenz Farm. Later, however, Wurzian expressed mixed feelings about the special course for agents he attended: "I learned much about things I had previously never imagined. We practiced crazy things and at the end we carried out the maddest four-day exercise: we weren't allowed to sleep and had only one meal per day. The time was broken down into sequences of two hours of physical work and one hour of mental work, the whole thing lasting 96 hours. Anyone who fell asleep was kicked off the course. They didn't catch me, so I passed the test. But I was never able to use what I had learned, during the war or afterwards. Thank God! In spite of everything I learned much that was new, which interested me, especially those things that had to do with water and ship sabotage. Many things seemed too primitive to me, however, and I believed that I could design and build more practical versions. They had the most wonderful multipurpose explosive cable, but I couldn't imagine for the life of me what to do with it. Was one supposed to wrap the cable around a warship and then set it off with a clockwork detonator? At best that would knock the dishes from the table onto the floor, but it could never crack the ship's thick iron side. The jiu-jitsu and karate I learned there were also interesting, but I couldn't imagine what use they would be to me as a diver."[16] Wurzian's vision was one of underwater warfare by lone warriors and went far beyond what was offered, thus his diary ended laconically: "The *Brandenburg* Division, as versatile as it was, soon bored me."[17]

After all his fruitless appeals to the various authorities, Wurzian realized that the *Abwehr* offered the most suitable platform from which to realize his idea of a German combat diver force. Finally he left his artillery unit to join the *Abwehr*. Effective 27 April 1943 he became a member of the 3rd Company of the 5th "*Brandenburg*" Training Regiment.[18] Unfortunately for Wurzian, however, he joined the *Abwehr* at a time when the *Brandenburg* Division was breaking up and *Abwehr* chief Canaris had already lost much of his influence. In November 1942, the *Brandenburg* Regiment, which by then had reached division strength, became "Special Unit *Brandenburg*" and in April 1943 the "*Brandenburg* Division". The increase in size also saw the beginning of a "normalization" process, which meant that while the *Brandenburgers* still had the potential for commando operations, they were increasingly used in the infantry role like normal troops. The final stage of this development and thus the official release from commando operations came on 1 April 1943, when the unit was officially removed from the *Abwehr* and the *Brandenburgers* placed under the command of the *Wehrmacht* operations staff. Wurzian's 5th Regiment was the only unit spared the normalization process. Initially it remained with the *Abwehr* under the name "(Training) Regiment *Kurfürst*", until in 1944 the organization was largely absorbed by the Reich Central Security Office.[19]

Created from the last fragment of the *Brandenburg* Division, Alfred von Wurzian's "Regiment *Kurfürst*" was not a unit in the actual sense, rather it was more a file card core regiment, in which personnel files were administered while the personnel themselves had been detached to various units and fronts for one-man and small-unit commando operations. All of the instructors from the *Abwehr*'s combat school at Quenz Lake had been sent to the "Regiment *Kurfürst*" along with other highly qualified specialists and experts who could be used to recruit and train spies, saboteurs and special combat troops. The "Regiment *Kurfürst*" did not conduct its own combat missions, and it would not be accurate to say that it carried on the traditions of the *Brandenburg* Division in the *Abwehr* after the former was normalized. In modern parlance the "Regiment *Kurfürst*" would be characterized as the *Abwehr*'s "power center". As specialists, the "*Kurfürsten*" were much sought after following the war and were recruited by the western allies for their own services. Those members of the "Regiment *Kurfürst*" captured and identified by the Russians had it much worse. Very few of them left the Bautzen camp alive.

CHAPTER FOUR

COMBAT DIVER
WITH THE ABWEHR

During his training at Quenz Farm, in February 1943 Wurzian also began working with Neumeyer to design the equipment to be used by the future German combat diver force. In addition to breathing equipment and fins, a combat diver would also need a watertight watch and navigation instruments like a compass and depth gauge. Also required was a suit to prevent rapid cooling. In addition to the diver's personal equipment, the type of explosives to be used was also an important question. What was the maximum weight of explosives a diver could transport over a long distance underwater, and what was the best way to securely attach the explosives to the ship? Many questions arose and were discussed by Wurzian and Neumeyer.

Wurzian was provided with an assistant to help with the development and testing of new equipment. He was *Gefreite* Richard Reimann of the *Brandenburg* Regiment. Their first task was to determine which existing products of German industry could be used and which items of equipment had to be developed from the ground up.

Wurzian was able to make use of some materials already at hand: the Dräger Company of Lübeck was already providing the *Wehrmacht* with breathing and diving equipment and it was selected to equip the combat divers with breathing equipment and goggles. At the instigation of the *Abwehr*, in early 1943 Dräger began further development of the oxygen circulation system and greatly improved a number of its functions. For example, in May 1943 the layout of the breathing hoses and other parts of the system was made more streamlined. A patent addendum dated September 1943 describes an improvement in the valves designed to make breathing easier. By the end of 1943 Dräger's oxygen circulation system had reached a form which would remain unchanged until the end of the war. The oxygen bottles, normally made of steel, posed a bigger problem. Ideally they should have been made entirely of light metal, because of the threat posed by magnetic mines. Steel tanks could also affect the compass. By that stage of the war aluminum was already in short supply in Germany and so Wurzian turned to the light metal used by the air force to make oxygen bottles for high-altitude aircraft.

The Semperit rubber company of Vienna was supposed to produce swim fins for the German combat divers. In the early 1940s swim fins were almost unknown and were viewed in many quarters as a curiosity rather than a swimming aid. The basic concept of the swim fin went back many centuries, but it was not until 1937 that the Frenchman Louis de Corlieu produced the first effective design.[20] Hans Hass picked up on the idea and had Semperit produce several modified examples for his expeditions. Hass anticipated the future market success of swim fins and their significance in the sporting and military fields. He envisaged large-scale production by Semperit and planned a company of his own company as a source of revenue for his research plans. He held the license rights for the German Reich and Semperit was his exclusive producer. On 10 February 1943 Department II/T (Mines Section)[21] contacted Semperit to ask if quantity production of swim fins was under way and enquire about the patent situation in Germany. Semperit replied that no production of swim fins was currently possible due to a shortage of raw India rubber and that to date only a few provisional samples had been produced for the Hass expeditions. At the beginning of March 1943, Dept. II/T placed an initial order with Semperit for 230 pairs of swim fins and designated the order as "priority". This gave the necessary impetus to production, and by July 1943 Semperit was able to begin deliveries of swim fins to the *Abwehr*. The shortage of raw materials resulted in production problems, however, and most of the fins used by German combat divers were made by the Italian Pirelli company. It was the same with other equipment: for the most part, the equipment used by German combat divers was of Italian origin.

In his search for suitable diving suits Wurzian came upon the Continental company of Hanover. Continental had begun production of protective rubber suits for long-distance and competitive swimmers in the 1920s. The existing suit was too thin, however, and tore easily, therefore it had to be made more robust for use by military divers. Here again, shortages of raw India rubber made themselves felt and production difficulties were predictable.

One of the most difficult problems to solve was that of navigation instruments. A compass and depth gauge were as vital to a combat diver as a watch, however these instruments had to be both watertight and easy to read in dark and murky water

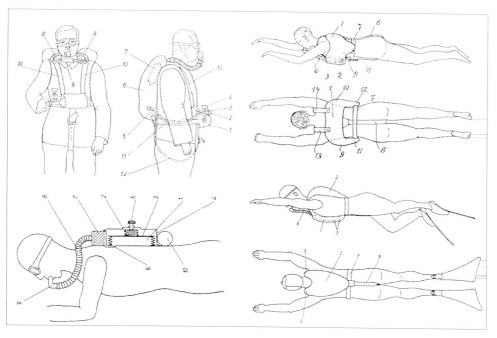

As the patent drawings document, from 1943 Dräger pursued development of the "counter-lung" in several stages. These design changes, combined with swim fins, turned it into a capable swim-diving system. Top left is the basic model, top right an improvement in the swimming posture, bottom left reduced breathing resistance through spring-assist, bottom right streamlined shape in combination with fins and mask. The last two development stages were never produced because of war-related production difficulties.

and at night. As well, the glass could not fog up in cold water and had to be thick enough to withstand blows. Of course the instruments had to function regardless of attitude to the maximum degree possible.

As there were no suitable instruments on the German market at that time, Wurzian and Neumeyer devised a mechanical watch and compass in a watertight plexiglass housing. This rather bulky device was then strapped to the diver's left arm and was used as an interim solution until better, more suitable instruments were developed.

At the end of April 1943 Wurzian and Reimann were working on the question of a depth gauge when they were directed to give a demonstration of their progress to date in the Olympic pool in Berlin. The reason for the order was a visit to the *Abwehr* by two Italian officers, Commander Prince Junio Valerio Borghese and Colonel Masciulli.[22] Borghese was a very successful submarine commander who had been placed in charge of the underwater section of the *Decima Flottiglia Mas*

(10th Motor Torpedo Boat Flotilla, originally just *Decima Mas*), which was also responsible for the planning, raising, training and deployment of the Italian Navy's small unit combat forces. The Italian officer was in Berlin for an exchange of ideas on ship sabotage equipment with Italy's German ally. In their dealings with their German allies, the Italians had so far proceeded under the principle "show them something, but not everything". Borghese later wrote that "we were to reveal secrets to our allies that had probably already been discovered by the enemy, but not those that appeared to be still intact."[23]

Wurzian and Reimann, who knew nothing about the knowledge being withheld by their Italian guests, proudly displayed their provisional equipment in the Olympic aquatic center and carried out a simulated underwater attack in the swimming pool. Borghese was little impressed: "They spoke of units of 100, battalions, indeed even of divisions of naval assault troops! From what I saw, however, I became convinced that the Germans barely grasped the rudiments of the underwater secret weapon. They had nothing to compare with our guided torpedoes or limpet charges. On the other hand they were very far advanced in the field of sabotage on land."

Borghese therefore decided to reveal the secrets of the Italian combat divers and their equipment to the Germans in exchange for German know-how in above-water sabotage. He wrote, "Based on my authority, I reached an agreement with the senior German officials to send a number of German soldiers on a *Decima Mas* training course so that they could later serve as instructors in Germany. Further, we traded Italian underwater breathing apparatus and free swimming suits for plastic explosives and other useful things the Germans had."[24]

In fact Italy possessed a major lead in underwater sabotage technology. Even before the First World War Italy had set up a small training camp for underwater saboteurs, where they were taught how to place explosive charges underwater and escape undetected. The history of modern small-unit tactics in naval warfare began in this Italian camp in 1918 when Major Rafaele Rossetti designed the first manned torpedo. It was no suicide weapon, however. A slender torpedo, almost seven meters long, it was powered by compressed air and guided by two divers sitting on it. The torpedo carried several mines which the divers could attach to a ship's hull after penetrating an enemy harbor. They would then set time detonators and head for home on their torpedo. The divers wore masks but as yet no breathing equipment, as the Italian navy still considered the oxygen circulation system too dangerous. The human torpedoes first saw action late in the First World War. On 31 October 1918 two Italian officers, Rafaele Rossetti and Rafaelle Paolucci, penetrated the port of Pola under cover of darkness and sank the Austrian battleship *Viribus Unitis* with limpet mines.

The Italians' next opportunity to employ combat divers did not come until 1935, when Mussolini sent his troops into defenseless Ethiopia. His fear of English intervention led him to order two experienced naval officers, Teseo Tesei and Elias Toschi, to set up a light and above all fast torpedo flotilla. Tesei and Toschi, both serving as submarine engineers at the naval base at La Spezia, established a secret seaside training camp where they built several underwater torpedo vehicles from a dozen different designs. In October 1935 they completed design work on the SLC (*Siluro a Lenta Corsa* = slow-running torpedo).

In contrast to Rossetti's very simple design, their device was to be a sort of submarine-torpedo combination. It consisted of a larger-diameter torpedo with a light superstructure housing two men in suits of rubberized cloth with oxygen breathing apparatus. The SLC was designed to operate several meters below the surface, enabling it to penetrate an enemy harbor unseen. It was powered by a small electric motor which ran almost silently. As the explosives carrier's radius of action was little more than 20 kilometers, it had to be transported to a point near the target area by larger submarines. The crew then had to attach the explosive charge beneath a ship and then exit the harbor on the device, now minus its warhead. England did not intervene in the Ethiopian affair, however, and the SLC saw no action.

This specialized equipment demanded courageous crews, but after Italy's entry into the war they achieved several notable successes. Borghese commanded one of the submarines which served as carrier for the two-man torpedoes and he took part in several successful attacks on the ports of Gibraltar and Alexandria.

The successful raids on enemy ports by the Italian small unit forces attracted much attention, but the secret of the human torpedoes was not made public until June 1943, when the Berlin Illustrated News published the first photos of the Italian secret weapon. In 1942 the Italians initiated a second form of underwater sabotage. Instead of riding torpedoes, combat divers wearing fins set out from shore to attack ships in port or at anchor on the roadstead. This was the birth of what the media would henceforth refer to as the "frogman" because of the shape of his fins. This is something of a misnomer, as the frog swims with a type of breaststroke and not the up and down motion of a man wearing swim fins.

For Wurzian, Borghese's visit to the Olympic aquatic facility was cause both for slight disappointment and great joy: surprise and disillusionment because he had to divest himself of the notion that he had been first to conceive the combat diver, and joy because soon afterwards he and Reimann were ordered to train with the Italian combat divers. The pair set off for Italy at the end of July, and Wurzian was very curious to see first hand the Italian techniques and their equipment.

From Berlin they traveled to Rome, where they had to report to the local *Abwehr* office. In charge of the Rome office, called "*Abwehr* Squad 204", was

Rittmeister Erwein Count von Thun-Hohenstein.[25] In 1940, while serving in the *Brandenburg* Regiment, he had taken part in the preparations for "Operation Felix", the conquest of Gibraltar. Wounded, in early 1943 he was taken off active service with the *Brandenburgers* and, as his older brother was head of the *Abwehr* head office for Italy in Milan, he was ordered to the *Abwehr* office in Rome.

Erwein Count von Thun-Hohenstein was Wurzian and Reimann's disciplinary superior in Italy. The pair reported to the *Rittmeister*, originally from Vienna, and when Thun-Hohenstein told Wurzian of his experiences and plans force a German combat diver force, a relationship of friendship and trust soon developed between the two Austrians. This subsequently resulted in Wurzian having maximum freedom of action in setting up a German combat diver force – at least until the *Kriegsmarine* took over from the *Abwehr* in the spring of 1944, resulting in a new command structure.

Wurzian and Reimann stayed in Rome for several days, and they soon became aware of the restless mood of the people and especially the Italian officer corps. The cause for the Italians' mood was the almost unimpeded invasion of Sicily by Allied forces several days earlier. In war-weary Italy, where the Second World War had never been popular, the invasion of Sicily and the first air raids on Rome in mid-July 1943 produced consternation which soon turned into a revolutionary, almost panicky mood. The Grand Fascist Council had pledged its loyalty to Benito Mussolini on 24 July, but just one day later King Victor Emmanuel III had the Duce arrested. While the king and the new prime minister Pietro Badoglio officially declared that they intended to continue the war at the side of their German ally, they soon entered into secret negotiations with the Allies with the goal of achieving a ceasefire.

Wurzian and Reimann were in Rome during these days of upheaval and began to sense the prevailing mood. Displeasure with the war and the Italians' subliminal desire for a ceasefire became very clear during a supper with Italian naval officers attended by Wurzian and Thun-Hohenstein. Thun-Hohenstein quickly grasped the situation and recognized the danger of an imminent bale-out by their ally. The next day he telegraphed a report to *Abwehr* headquarters in Berlin and received a placatory reply. No, Berlin did not anticipate a breach of the coalition by the Italians and they assured Thun-Hohenstein that the mood of the people would soon improve. They had been forewarned though, and were preparing countermeasures. In the end, however, Thun-Hohenstein's warning was to prove correct.[26]

The secret negotiations by the Italian government in fact led to a ceasefire between Italy and the Allies on 3 September 1943. On 8 September Badoglio went on the radio to announce the ceasefire. The prepared German countermeasures went into effect at once: Italian forces in Italy, southern France and the Balkans were disarmed and taken prisoner, and German troops occupied Rome.

Italy was effectively divided by the military situation. The German 10th Army under *Generaloberst* Heinrich von Vietinghoff succeeded in establishing a continuous defense line across the Italian mainland north of Naples. In the months that followed, the line was further fortified and was dubbed the "Gustav Position" by German propaganda. It extended from the mouth of the Garigliano on the Tyrrhenian Sea to the mouth of the Sangro on the Adriatic.

On 13 October the Allied-occupied anti-fascist southern half of Italy under Badoglio declared war on Germany. In the north Mussolini, who in mid-September had been freed by German paratroops and a team of SS commandos, established the Italian Social Republic, a fascist counter-government.

CHAPTER FIVE

TRAINING WITH THE GAMMA COMBAT DIVERS

Alfred von Wurzian and Richard Reimann were with the Italian combat divers when the ceasefire came. As per orders, on 1 August 1943 they had joined the Italian combat diver unit at Quercianella-Sonnino, about 10 km south of Livorno. There, in a former resort community, was the field camp of the so called "Gamma Unit". The combat divers' headquarters was at the Livorno naval academy in San Leopoldo, which also offered a swimming pool.

In charge of training the combat divers was the Italian Lieutenant Eugen Wolk, an outstanding athlete and a very experienced swimmer. Wolk, whom Wurzian characterized as very composed, deliberate and quiet man with piercing blue eyes and an almost naïve philosophy of life, was a Russian German born in Chernigov, Ukraine. His ancestors had immigrated via Riga and Minsk to Chernigov in the 19th Century, however the revolution of 1917 led the family to return to Germany. They initially emigrated to Dresden, but as asylum seekers were not very welcome in postwar Germany, the Wolk family moved on via Istanbul to Rome, arriving there in 1919. Quite unlike in Germany, their reception there was very friendly, and Eugen's father selected a naval officer's career for his son. Wolk attended the naval academy and in Livorno got to know director Angelo Belloni. Belloni was one of the leading Italian experts in diving technology and had already begun theorizing about an Italian combat diver unit in the style of the later Gamma unit. Wolk put Belloni's ideas into practice and further developed them.

Wolk's nickname was "Egli", and as he spoke excellent German he served as liaison between the Italian unit and the two Germans. Wolk recognized Wurzian

Training director of the Italian combat divers, Eugen Wolk.

*The "Model 49" oxygen cir-
culation device used by Italian
combat divers was a pendulum
breathing device with attached
mask. The twin oxygen tanks enabled a diver to stay underwater
for up to two hours.*

as his equal when it came to diving technology, but Wolk possessed a clear lead when it came to its possible military applications. The Italians were not much more advanced in basic equipment – breathing devices, fins and suit – but they were more advanced with respect to navigation instruments, explosives and offensive tactics.

The Italian combat divers had already carried out a number of successful operations and amassed valuable experience. The first operation by Italian combat divers took place in the port of Gibraltar in mid-July 1942 – almost the same day that Wurzian had demonstrated the new diving equipment to the admiral commanding the Aegean at the mole in Piraeus.

In the weeks that followed a relationship of partnership developed between Wurzian and Wolk, and Wolk endeavored to convey as much knowledge as possible about equipment and tactics to the two *Abwehr* men. The mutual learning between Wolk and Wurzian went so far that Wolk mainly spoke German to Wurzian, in order to practice the language, and Wurzian tried to answer in Italian in order to improve his knowledge of that language. Wurzian has fond memories of this period: "Finally I was able to again swim and dive, as long as my oxygen allowed, in the azure-blue waters of the Mediterranean, and there I learned much that was new."[27]

The Italian breathing system was a simple oxygen circulation device based on an English design and was somewhat inferior to the new Dräger systems. Initially it was a rebreather with just one combined hose for in- and exhaling, manufactured by the Pirelli company. The advantage of the rebreather system was its simplicity and the intensive removal of carbon-dioxide, as the breathing air in part passed twice through the cartridge filter. This system did, however, have the disadvantage of an excessively large dead space, especially in combination with a full-face mask.

The breathing tube ended in a full-face mask with one large (Model G 50) or two small (model 49/bis) eyepieces. During combat operations, when long distances had to be swum and only a short dive was necessary, eye protection was usually dispensed with and just a nose clip was used. The nose clip enabled the equalization of pressure in the frontal sinuses and inner ear while diving. In the breathing device's mouthpiece was a small valve. This was closed when the mouthpiece was not used while swimming, to prevent water from entering the breathing sack.

The fins used by the Italian combat divers were also from Pirelli. They were the standard commercial model which, on account of their success, continued to be sold for years after the war under the product name *Superga*. The fins were asymmetrical in shape, similar to a fish's tail, and had an open shoe part. A heel strap was used to mount them onto the sturdy rubber laced shoes which the combat diver wore over his thin India rubber suit.

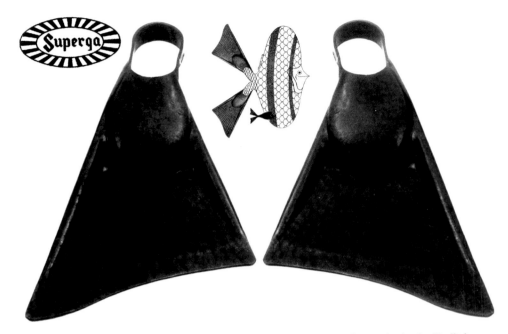

"Superga" brand swim fins were patterned after fish fins and remained in production by Pirelli for many years after the war.

As combat divers were often in the water for hours at a time, they required a special suit to protect them from the cold. The so-called "half dry" diving suit was also made by Pirelli. It was made of thin black rubber with a laced outer protective covering made of cotton. This protection was especially important, for if the rubber suit was damaged its heat retention capabilities were quickly lost. This could be very dangerous to the combat diver, as he faced the risk of hypothermia if required to swim a long distance to shore. The two-piece suit was made up of a hoodless jacket and pants with feet. The pants and jacket overlapped in the belly area and were rolled together. A rubber band was also often used to stick the two together.

Woolen underwear was often worn beneath the thin rubber suit. Close-fitting cuffs on the wrists and collar restricted water circulation. On entering the water, the diver had to loosen the neck cuff with one hand and submerge up to his chin. Water ran into the suit until it was completely filled. Then the neck cuff was closed again and the mission could begin. The water allowed into the suit was slowly warmed by the diver's body temperature, creating a thin warming insulating layer between body and suit. Normally, with the cuffs in place, this insulating layer was lost, but very slowly. If the suit was torn, however, there was a constant exchange

A German sea commando wearing Pirelli breathing equipment and nose clamp. The cock for closing the breathing hose is clearly visible. Eye protection was usually not worn, and later the nose clamp fell into disuse.

of water and the effectiveness of the insulating layer was severely reduced. In combination with grease applied to the skin, the suit itself provided a significant degree of protection against cold.

A foam-rubber suit was later introduced for use in colder waters like the North Sea, the Baltic and inland waterways. A special foam-rubber hood could also be used to keep the head warm. The small air pockets in the foam rubber reduced its thermal conductivity. The combat diver had an unorthodox emergency solution for warming the insulating layer of water during lengthy missions: he urinated in the suit. This was not very appealing, but it was effective.

 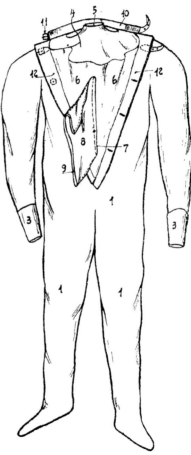

The so-called "Belloni dive suit. The photo shows how the wearer had to spread the head opening with his hands in order to force his head through. On the right is a drawing with the closeable entry opening at chest level.

A second variant was the so-called "Belloni dive suit".[28] Named for its inventor, it consisted of a much thicker, more robust cotton webbing worn under a rubber suit. Putting on the hoodless Belloni suit required some dexterity: it was a one-piece affair and was completely closed except for the openings on the two sleeves and the collar. These openings were provided with cuffs of thin India rubber which sealed the suit. There was a larger opening at chest level, which was used for entry. The diver stuck his feet through the opening then slipped his arms and head into the suit. Stretching the neck opening with his hands, he slipped his head through. Finally he forced his two arms into the sleeves. A small wooden disc with a groove in its outer edge, over which the outer lip of the entrance was wound and secured with a rubber ring, sealed the entrance slit. This "winding" was an exercise which the divers also had to master underwater. The entire entrance area at chest height could then be protected with a buttoned cotton web.

In order to provide the necessary freedom of movement while putting on and taking off the suit, the portion over the upper body was relatively loose-fitting. Consequently all air had to be removed from the suit before submerging, otherwise it would possess excessive buoyancy. In the beginning the air was removed in the water – the diver entered the water until it reached chest level, then loosened the neck cuff allowing the air inside to escape. Later the suit was fitted with an additional valve, which the diver used to suck the air from the suit before entering the water. A set of woolen underwear or even an entire uniform could be worn under the suit. Because of its robustness and its good insulation, the Belloni "dry suit" offered significant advantages compared to the thinner "half dry suit". It was, however, quite stiff, and the folds caused by sucking out the air created pressure points on the skin and were vulnerable to wearing through. Consequently the Belloni suit was usually used only when the diver had to spend long periods in the water, such as during underwater searches, the SLC torpedo procedure or other time-limited work under water.

Regardless of the type of suit, the combat diver wore on his head a thin cloth cap onto which had been sewed a camouflage net. Algae or other things resembling flotsam could be affixed to this and serve as camouflage. The camouflage netting was pulled down over the face during the approach to the target, concealing the swimmer's pale skin and making him almost invisible against the water's surface. Charcoal was also sometimes used to blacken the face.

During the approach to the target the swimmer propelled himself through the water with undetectable, silent fin movements, swimming on his back or side so as to keep his objective or aiming point on the shore in sight. As well, when swimming on his back the swimmer's ears were frequently under water. This was an advantage, especially at night, because of water's excellent sound-conducting properties, which allowed him to hear screw noises from a greater distance.

The only weapon the swimmer carried with him was a combat knife, which was attached to his diving equipment's belly belt by means of a carbine hook. It was seen primarily as a close-combat weapon for use on land.

Wurzian was especially interested by the instruments and underwater explosives used by the Italian combat divers, as the German developments in this area were still in their initial stages. The Italians used watches, compasses and depth gauges made by the Italian watchmaking company Officine Panerai, which supplied precision instruments to the Italian navy. In 1936 Panerai began developing instruments for Italian combat divers.

The watch used by the combat divers was Panerai's "Radiomir" model, with a manual winder and a running time of about 48 hours. A highly-illuminating special mixture on its hands and dial face made it very easy to read and it was also very robust.[29] The secret of its readability, even in extreme darkness, was the use of a special substance – a mixture of phosphorescent zinc sulfide and radium bromide. Relatively large, with a diameter of 47 mm, and with a pillow-shaped housing, the first Radiomirs had no markings at all on their black dial face. In the beginning they were assembled from a housing made exclusively by Rolex in Geneva and a clockwork mechanism. The cannon was held in place by screws, and through the use of a special lever mechanism a later version was watertight to a depth of 200 meters – an absolute record for that time which meant a high safety reserve.

Watches were vitally important for coordinating dive work and the precise setting of time detonators, but so were depth gauges and compasses. The depth gauge was important for monitoring depth. The Panerai devices measured the actual depth using the surrounding pressure. The first simple models worked on the principle of depth measurement by means of a Bourdon tube. While very accurate, they were only suitable to a depth of about 10 meters. An improved model with a rubber membrane and mechanical lever gear provided indications by pointer and dial face.

A compass was indispensable for orientation underwater. Panerai therefore developed various types of compass whose outstanding feature was their relative insensitivity to large metal masses such as ships' hulls and torpedo nets. The magnet system in the compass was suspended in an oily fluid, which absorbed shocks and damped the movement of the pointer. The first compass rose dial face type could only be read clearly in a horizontal position. Pointer illumination was improved by a coat of radium paint or Radiomir small glass tube. In many cases, however, the illumination was so bright that the diver had to cover the dial face with a cloth or mud to avoid being seen.

This still relatively conventional compass design had two main drawbacks: first the compass had to be in an exactly horizontal position to be read and second the

The "Radiomir" model watch by Panerai was the standard type used by combat divers. The presence of the maker's name on the dial face is very unusual. The owner, Günter Heyden, engraved his initials on the back. Also of interest is the typical Rolex winder. (Photo: Knirim, Konrad: Military Watches)

risk that the strong illumination needed underwater might be seen by watchful eyes above water, betraying the user's position. Over time, therefore, Panerai modified the design. First they developed a conical version which could be read even in a tilted position, and later an opaque cap with a viewing window was added.

The depth gauges and compasses were fitted with a large, semi-spherical plexiglass cap and could be worn over the diving suit like a watch by using a long armband made of oiled leather. The leather armband was later replaced by a synthetic material. There was also a combined compass-depth gauge in a common housing.[30] A watertight underwater flashlight powered by batteries completed the equipment. It had a special mechanism to prevent inadvertent switching-on during a diving operation.

As there were no comparable instruments in Germany, German combat divers were later equipped with this Italian equipment – when it could be obtained. The Radiomir watches used by combat divers have become prized collectors items.

The Italian Gamma swimmers used two main types of explosives: small 2-kilogram charges which were attached to a ship's hull by means of a suction cup, and the somewhat larger 4.5-kilogram charge which could be attached to a ship's bilge keel by means of two screw clamps.

Despite many efforts at deception, the Allies soon identified the causes of the explosions and began dragging a steel cable along the hull bottoms of ships before they sailed. In response to this, explosive charges were fitted with a small skid over which the cable could slide without catching. The Allies in turn began using divers of their own to examine ships' hulls before they sailed. The response was to modify the charges so that they would explode if an attempt was made to remove them.

Each combat diver carried up to six of these small charges on his harness. This was more effective than transporting a single large charge and had the same destructive power. As well there was the reassurance that the failure of a single detonator would not jeopardize the entire mission. Time detonators were equipped with a special mechanism, however, and as the war progressed they increasingly became a bottleneck which hampered many underwater operations.

While most of Wurzian and Reimann's time in Quercianella was spent learning to use the breathing apparatus and navigation instruments, they also dedicated a portion to practical maneuvers. After demonstrations by Italian instructors, the pair practiced exchanging breathing apparatus underwater and exiting the torpedo tube of a submerged submarine. Many years later Wurzian still had fond memories of those informative weeks at the Italian combat divers' camp. He observed that never again did he experience such comradeship and close bonds, where each respected and took responsibility for the other regardless of rank. This comradeship was born of the fact that underwater each had to and could blindly depend on the other. This atmosphere of trust also extended to normal duties above water.

Borghese later described the character qualities and the community of the Italian combat divers as follows: "Inflexible will, power of decision and endurance, disregard of danger, unwavering steadiness and unconditional commitment of one's own life for the fatherland. The most important quality, however, was silence, not only in regard to weapons, training, size and location of the unit or the names of comrades and superiors, but also in regard to membership in the unit. No one, not even one's own parents or wife, could know which special unit the volunteer had joined. In the 'Decima' one lived in a closed circle, cut off from outside influences. Political discussions, erroneous conclusions about an imminent end to the war, sudden enthusiasm over successes or depression over failures were unknown to us. For us there was just one thought, a burning objective, a goal: to prepare our men and equipment, to sharpen our spirit, in order to find a way to strike the heaviest blows against the enemy. This concept dominated everyone's thinking – the commander and the officers, the NCOs and seamen. We were all joined together by a bond much stronger than discipline. Respect for the worth and performance of the individual united us. The seamen 'felt' that the officers were their superiors, and at every opportunity, especially in the face of the enemy, the officers acted in such a way as to prove themselves worthy of their special position and spur their subordinates to vie in bravery and skill more through example than orders. This created the strongest ties and this enabled the men to perform outstanding feats."

The ceasefire announced by the Italian government on 8 September 1943 initially brought the cooperation between Wolk and Wurzian to an abrupt end. Wolk, who was taken completely by surprise by the ceasefire and had no idea how he should conduct himself, carried out the government's new orders, placing Wurzian and Reimann under guard in a tent for a time while waiting for further orders.

The situation that day was confused, and as Wurzian had no intention of taking any risks he and Reimann made plans to escape. They wanted to try to reach the German garrison in Livorno in order to wait for further developments in safer surroundings. Chance came to the aid of the two *Abwehr* men, for that evening Wolk, who was just as disoriented as Wurzian, ordered a soldier to drive a truck to Livorno to obtain further orders from the Italian post there and transport secret documents from Quercianella to Livorno in a safe. The headquarters of the Gamma divers was located there in the naval academy.

Wurzian, who by now understood the Italian language well, overheard Wolk's orders through the thin canvas of the tent, and it was clear to him that they could use this as an opportunity to escape. That evening Wurzian and Reimann heard the courier driver getting ready and the truck start. They quickly slit open the back of the tent with a knife, sprinted the few meters from the tent to the truck, and jumped beneath the cover over the vehicle's rear bed. A few minutes later the truck left the camp and headed for Livorno. The first part of the escape had succeeded and the drive was to present Wurzian with an especially valuable prize: in the back of the truck there was a black leather suitcase, which Wurzian opened and inspected immediately after leaving the camp. In their escape they had been unable to take anything with them, and they hoped that the case might contain food, arms or other things that might be useful in their flight. Wurzian was surprised, however, to find that there was nothing in the case but secret documents, design drawings and operating descriptions for Italian one-man submarines, similar to the later German 'Biber' (Beaver), and other Italian navy equipment.

The truck took the coast road and reached the outskirts of Livorno without stopping. The first time the vehicle stopped in Livorno, Wurzian and Reimann jumped out and hid in a niche in a wall. Wurzian took with him the suitcase containing the important documents.

By now it was night, and Wurzian could hear the sound of rifle shots over the sound of the truck's engine as it pulled away. Wurzian wasn't sure whether it was Italian soldiers celebrating the ceasefire or combat between German and Italian forces. As going farther into the city seemed unsafe, Wurzian and Reimann decided to remain in their hiding place outside the city until dawn and then make contact with German troops.

Wurzian and Reimann circled round Livorno and then turned north, parallel to the road to Pisa. There they encountered German troops on their way to secure Pisa airport. Wurzian and Reimann joined the troops and subsequently arrived at Pisa airport. One day after the Italian surrender the situation there was still uncertain, but the airfield was firmly in German hands.

Wurzian had just one thought: no matter how the situation in Italy developed, he had to get his suitcase full of stolen secret documents out of Italy as quickly as possible and present it to the *Abwehr* in Berlin. But neither Wurzian nor Reimann had any kind of papers on them identifying who they were. On his collar Reimann did have a small inconspicuous pin, which together with a codeword was intended to identify him to informed persons as "an agent of the *Abwehr* on a special mission"; but the German troops in Pisa were unaware of this recognition sign and it was thus worthless. Wurzian was able, however, to convince the airfield commander of the importance and urgency of his mission. The officer in fact arranged for a flight from Rome to Vicenza to stop in Pisa to pick up Wurzian and his valuable cargo. As there were only a few empty seats on the aircraft, Reimann was forced to stay behind in Pisa and try to find another way back to Berlin.

After landing at Vicenza, Wurzian boarded another aircraft and finally reached Munich. There the game began all over again: he had to convince the authorities that he was on an extremely urgent mission and had to transport the case to Berlin without delay. This was anything but a simple task, for Wurzian had no papers to confirm that he was a member of the military secret service. To the airfield commandant at Munich-Riem he was just a soldier in simple khaki uniform with no rank badges, with a black leather case full of secret documents in his hand. In the end it was thanks to Wurzian's powers of persuasion and the magic power of the term "*Abwehr* man" that a courier cabin was made available to him on a train from Munich to Berlin. In his dark, locked cabin, Wurzian caught up on two days of missed sleep.

Wurzian arrived in Berlin on 13 September and immediately reported to Senior Engineer Neumeyer. Neumeyer excitedly examined the plans in the suitcase and realized at once that they were extremely valuable. As a detailed examination of the documents would take several days, he placed Wurzian on well-earned special leave until then.

Just two days later Neumeyer telephoned Wurzian and informed him that they would be meeting with Admiral Canaris, head of the *Abwehr*, on the following day. This was Wurzian's second and last meeting with the often difficult to assess

Abwehr chief. The first meeting had taken place half a year earlier, immediately after Wurzian joined the *Brandenburgers*. Wurzian now found himself sitting in an office on the Bendlerstrasse with Canaris, Neumeyer and a large number of other *Abwehr* officers.

Canaris initially made only brief mention of the plans in the case, observing almost as an aside that they were certainly of great worth. But he went on to say that he didn't believe that there was sufficient time to build and test such specialized equipment and in particular to form a specialized unit like the Italian *Decima Mas*. On the one hand he justified this by declaring that this method of fighting was beyond the scope of military intelligence, and on the other by the fact that following the Italian government's ceasefire the commander of *Decima Mas*, Count Borghese, speaking for most of his officers, had declared himself ready to continue fighting at Germany's side. Thus this Italian special unit was available to Germany anyway.

As the meeting progressed, Canaris wanted to hear about Wurzian's experiences with the "Gamma" combat divers in Livorno and his estimation of their military capabilities and reliability. Wurzian described his very lasting, positive impression of Wolk's unit, after which Canaris ordered him to return to Italy immediately. Wurzian was to proceed to La Spezia, where he was to serve as liaison officer between the *Abwehr* and the *Decima Mas* until further notice. According to Canaris, there was an agreement between the armed forces high command and the navy that the *Abwehr* should be responsible for contact with the *Decima Mas* and therefore had to assume all further responsibilities such as providing the unit with rations and pay. Wurzian was assigned this task as he had already worked closely with elements of *Decima Mas* and knew its inner structure and some of its officers.

CHAPTER SIX

LIAISON OFFICER TO THE DECIMA MAS

On 22 September, only about two weeks after his escape from Quercianella, Wurzian traveled back to Italy. As he did so he had a very uneasy feeling, for he had no idea how he would be received by the Italians. Had Wolk discovered his theft of the secret documents, and if so would he blame him for the coup de main?

No mention of the lost documents was made after his arrival in La Spezia, and neither Wolk nor Borghese ever brought it up. Wurzian was astonished. Even later, after the war, Wurzian was never able to determine whether Wolk had in fact known nothing about the loss of the secret documents or had accepted it in silence.[31] In fact, from the moment Wurzian left Canaris' office, the subject of the documents was never raised again, neither by the navy or the *Abwehr*. Whether Canaris intentionally kept them to himself or they were forgotten in an archive, in any case it seems certain that had they been put to use immediately, the Italian design plans captured by Wurzian would surely have accelerated the formation of a German special underwater unit.

Prior to leaving for Italy, Wurzian had been promoted to the rank of *Feldwebel* and decorated with the Iron Cross, Second Class. In La Spezia he met Wolk and Borghese, and his comrade Richard Reimann too. Reimann had come to La Spezia direct from Pisa. The headquarters of the *Decima Mas* in the navy arsenal was now also the "Gamma" unit's base.

One of Wurzian's first official acts in La Spezia was to take part in a parade by the *Decima Mas* and convey a message of greeting from Canaris. He mastered the task in his now acceptable Italian, praised the bravery of the Italian navy and promised the support of the German armed forces. At a subsequent reception Wurzian met other command-level officers of the *Decima Mas*.

In the weeks that followed, Wurzian considered how to pursue his idea of establishing a German combat diver unit on the Italian model. Borghese had offered to place a group of Italian "Gamma" divers from Wolk's unit under his command, but this did not fit Wurzian's plans. He wanted a German unit under the umbrella of the *Abwehr*. During his last visit, Wurzian had not detected any great interest in the idea on the part of Canaris. Training a group of *Abwehr* men as combat divers to undertake acts of sabotage was surely reasonable, but an entire regiment – no. Canaris had other ideas in mind for his military secret service. Whether Canaris would even have been able to form such a new unit under his command at the end of 1943 is a question that must be evaluated openly and skeptically. By then Canaris had long been in the crossfire of the SS, had lost his standing with Adolf Hitler and much of his influence. In autumn 1943 Canaris was a man on the verge of losing his power. Wurzian began putting his ideas for a German combat diver unit, its possible formation, and areas of operations, down on paper. His descriptions of the operational possibilities of combat divers, further fed by discussions with Wolk, ranged from sabotage operations against fixed objects like coastal batteries, bridges, locks and harbors, to the affixing of explosive charges to enemy ships in foreign ports. Wurzian's inspiration for the latter was a newsreel showing a German submarine against the New York skyline.

Delivery of a number of combat divers to an enemy port by submarine or disguised ship and the placing of explosive charges on ships scheduled to depart was already technically feasible. The explosive charges would be fitted with a distance-measuring device similar to the odometer in a car, so that they would not explode until the ship had traveled a certain, previously set, distance – for example 500 nautical miles. The device had to be designed so that its small propeller, or screw, did not begin to turn until the ship had reached a certain speed, about 15 knots, to prevent the propeller being turned by the harbor current. The ship would sink on the high sea, far from the harbor and the "scene of the crime". No one would be able to make a connection, for the explosive charges would all be set differently – some would explode after 200 nautical miles, others not until 500 or 800 nautical miles. The enemy would have to assume that the ship had been torpedoed or struck a mine. No one would conclude that it was the result of an act of sabotage in port.[32]

Another aspect in favor of distance detonators was the idea that a ship sunk close to port could be refloated quickly and its cargo possibly salvaged. As well, there could be diplomatic complications if an attack took place in a neutral port like Gibraltar and not in international waters.

Another of Wurzian's ideas was the construction of "combat diver bunkers" as part of the Atlantic Wall. A series of bunkers, 30 kilometers apart, were to be built on the coastline. Each would have just one common entrance/exit beneath the surface of the water. Each bunker would contain provisions, clothing and equipment for eight combat divers. The divers would occupy the bunkers when the invasion started and use them as bases for attacks on ships, landing craft and landing platforms.[33]

For Wurzian this was a very productive time, for "I was constantly coming up with new ideas, one after the other."[34] Wurzian's dossier went to *Abwehr* headquarters in Berlin, but there was no feedback. Wurzian later recalled: "They simply left me alone, without giving me any support whatsoever, their motto being: if it isn't helping anything, it surely won't hurt anything either. And those with whom I discussed my ideas just laughed derisively."[35]

All of October passed, and Wurzian's ideas first began to become reality when Commander von Kamptz-Borken arrived in La Spezia to relieve him as liaison officer between the German armed forces and the *Decima Mas*. Wurzian briefed the officer on the situation first hand and took the opportunity to sell his ideas. Kamptz-Borken was impressed and promised to pass them on to the navy command. And in fact at the beginning of December 1943 a committee of German naval officers came to La Spezia to check out Wurzian's ideas and witness a diving demonstration by combat divers. The next night Wurzian and Reimann carried out a simulated attack on a warship in the harbor and remained undetected, even though the lookouts on the deck of the ship had been forewarned and the surrounding waters were kept under close observation. The demonstration was a complete success, and the impressed committee returned to Berlin, promising that they would be hearing back soon.

After the successful demonstration, Wurzian now was justifiably hopeful that he might be given a number of soldiers for training and be allowed to form a German combat diver unit. Then, several days later, Wurzian received the encouraging news that a group of navy personnel would be arriving in early January 1944. In addition to members of the *Kriegsmarine*, however, the first training course would also include men from the *Abwehr* and the *Waffen-SS*.

The assignment of navy personnel took place at the direction of Vice-Admiral Eberhardt Weichold, who in 1943 had been given the task of forming a small battle unit. For this task Grand Admiral Dönitz had made him his special representative in the naval operations staff. Command of the *Kriegsmarine* had passed from Grand Admiral Raeder to Grand Admiral Dönitz, former commander of the submarine arm. In addition to reorganizing the units of the navy, Dönitz had also promised to form a small battle unit. Aware that Hellmuth Heye – now a Rear Admiral and

The Kriegsmarine committee sent to La Spezia to examine Alfred von Wurzian's combat diver idea, December 1943.

chief-of-staff of Naval Group Headquarters North[36] and of fleet headquarters – favored such a special unit, he actually had him in mind as commander. Dönitz later wrote: "During meetings with Rear Admiral Balzer, the navy's head of personnel, at the beginning of February 1943 I expressed the wish that Rear Admiral Heye be relieved and placed at my disposal. He was to form units and gather equipment for a naval small battle force. Such 'small battle resources' did not as yet exist in the German navy – Heye seemed to me to be suited for the new task, because he was full of ideas, but the head of personnel convinced me that he was needed as fleet headquarters chief-of-staff and suggested Vice-Admiral Weichold in his place. He had served effectively as head of the naval academy and First Naval Staff Officer in fleet headquarters. Later he had been assigned as liaison officer to the Italian navy. In his new task, the formation of small battle units, Weichold essentially limited himself to determining their theoretical principles. It was also unfortunate for him that at the time of our activities the close ties between the naval high command and armaments minister Speer and German industry, which later proved particularly advantageous in the practical formation of small battle units, did not as yet exist."[37]

Eugen Wolk had meanwhile found new quarters for his Italian combat divers in the southern Dolomite Mountains: Valdagno, a small city in a beautiful valley at the foot of Mount Pasubio, near the famous spa town of Recoaro Terme.[38] The location offered suitable training facilities for the Gamma divers, and it was hoped that the special unit could better be kept secret there. It was there that the training course for the new German combat divers was also to be held, together with the Italian combat divers.

CHAPTER SEVEN

VALDAGNO - COMBAT DIVING AS A SPORTING CHALLENGE

Eugen Wolk and Alfred von Wurzian arrived in Valdagno in early December 1943. Wolk's unit consisted of about 80 Italian combat divers, and he had meanwhile named Luigi Ferraro as his deputy. Ferraro had carried out several extremely daring and successful operations in the summer of 1943. He sabotaged and sank several Allied ships in the Turkish ports of Alexandrette (present-day Iskenderun) and Mersina (present-day Mersin) while they were at anchor more than two kilometers offshore, loading chromium.

The German armed forces had taken control of the Agno Valley soon after the Italian ceasefire, in particular the object of the most strategic importance, the Lanifici Marzotto textile factories. From then on they produced uniform fabric for the German Ministry of Armaments and War Production almost exclusively. Soldiers of the 11th Special Purpose Air Signals Battalion (Motorized), a specialized radio unit of the *Luftwaffe*, had already arrived in Valdagno. The German commandant was headquartered in the former Casa del Fascio on the Piazza Dante and was subordinate to *Oberstleutnant* Trippe.[39]

The reason the combat divers went to Valdagno was the large, modern sporting facilities that influential textile entrepreneur Gaetano Marzotto had built for his workers on the left bank of the Agno River in the 1930s. He wanted to realize his vision of a model settlement, an ideal "social city", in Valdagno, which would include adequate facilities for his workers to enjoy their spare time. Marzotto built a large indoor swimming pool with six 25-meter lanes and diving tower, a large sports stadium and a gymnasium: essentially a complete private Olympic village.

Exterior view of the aquatic facility in Valdagno.

All sporting facilities had been taken over by the German commander's office and were now to serve as a new training facility for the combat divers.

The combat divers' officers lived in the Hotel Pasubio on the Piazza Cavour, while the men – this time with the Germans and Italians separated – were housed in commandeered school buildings and other quarters near the sporting facilities. While the Italian combat divers were under the overall command of and received their pay from the German military, their internal structure remained unchanged after the ceasefire. Despite their close proximity, any cooperation or exchange between the German and Italian combat divers took place almost exclusively between Wurzian and Wolk. Otherwise the two units were largely separate, both with regard to training and operations.[40]

To Valdagno also came the first German personnel to receive the so-called "sea fighter" training: men from the *Abwehr*, from the SS Reich Central Security Office, the navy, paratroopers and mountain infantry. With the first lot of about two dozen *Abwehr* men came *Hauptmann* Neitzert.[41] He became Wurzian's superior and the first commander of the newly-formed "Sea Commando Battalion *Brandenburg*". It was completely independent from the existing "Coastal Commando Battalion *Brandenburg*".

The individual groups could not have been more different. The *Abwehr* soldiers were all committed special forces, who in future would be used in the ship sabotage role. They had already received specialized *Abwehr* training at Quenz Farm and were mentally prepared for dangerous small unit missions. What they lacked was the physical fitness required by a combat diver, the specific sabotage-related technical knowledge and the proper techniques to be used with diving equipment. The first real combat diver missions would later be conducted almost exclusively by volunteers from their ranks.

The SS personnel sent for "sea fighter" training consisted of about a dozen demoted soldiers from the Oranienburg Special Missions Battalion, the probation company within the SS Commando Unit Center.[42] It was formed in autumn 1943 from elements of the 1st Company of the 502nd SS Light Infantry (Mot.)

Alfred von Wurzian with the first commander of the "Sea Commando Battalion Brandenburg", Hauptmann Fritz Neitzert (center) of the Abwehr.

Battalion, which had previously fought bloody battles against partisans in Croatia under *SS-Hauptsturmführer* Vessem. The constant anti-partisan warfare had worn down and desensitized the SS men. Those sent to Valdagno had been punished and demoted at the front for various reasons, and as stated identically and obliquely in their personnel files, they were expected to "redeem themselves for past crimes", which was another way of saying carry out a dangerous mission in place of the death sentence. By Hitler's order, the SS had its own military code separate from that of the *Wehrmacht*, and sentences could be handed down based on the values of the "Black Order". Some really were criminals, while others had committed only relatively minor offences against the strict honor code of the SS. An example of this was an *Oberscharführer* who stole a pig from a Croatian farmer and slaughtered it to silence his hunger. He was demoted and sentenced to death, but his sentence was commuted to "probation".

The SS soldiers on probation wore navy uniforms and the rank of "seaman", the lowest naval rank there was. This was because the convicted men were no longer worthy to wear the "honorable" SS uniform or an SS rank. With their conviction they had been completely thrown out of the SS, which considered itself an elite formation.[43] This fact was initially not known in Valdagno, where it was suspected that the SS men had volunteered for the "sea fighters" and had even gone so far as to give up their SS rank.

These SS men, who had been sentenced to death, were later involved in a disagreeable incident. They represented a constant problem, for when it came to discipline they were not subordinate to the commander of the Sea Commando Battalion, rather directly to the head of Dept. VI-S in the Reich Central Security Office, *SS-Sturmbannführer* Otto Skorzeny.[44] "Operation Alarich", the commando raid which freed Benito Mussolini from captivity on the Gran Sasso, had made Skorzeny a hero.[45] Skorzeny had German mass propaganda to thank for the duration and scale of his fame as it made him one of the most popular figures of the war inside and outside Germany. Hitler, too, had great sympathy for this roguish, daring officer, whose great size and scarred face, the result of duels during his student days, made a great physical impression. Skorzeny became Hitler's crisis manager: after Gran Sasso the Führer repeatedly gave him special missions and Skorzeny cultivated his direct links to Hitler, often bypassing his superiors and occasionally even the OKW.

In the postwar trials at Dachau, the chief prosecutor once called Skorzeny "the most dangerous man in Europe". Operating out of Reich Central Security Office Dept. VI "*SD-Ausland*", one of the office's largest departments led by *SS-Brigadeführer* Walter Schellenberg, *Sturmbannführer* Skorzeny was responsible for Group VI-S (Foreign Intelligence Service for Espionage and Intelligence Abroad).[46] In

April 1943, building on the "Special Course for Special Duties Oranienburg", he began forming a *Waffen-SS* organization similar to the *Brandenburg* units of the *Ausland/Abwehr* Office. Also placed under *Sturmbannführer* Skorzeny's command was the *Waffen-SS*' sabotage and agent school in Jagdschloss Friedenthal at Sachsen-hausen near Oranienburg, which performed a similar function to the *Abwehr*'s agent school at the farm on Quenz Lake. Friedenthal became Skorzeny's headquarters. In June 1943 the special course was reorganized into the "Special Unit for Special Duties Friedenthal" and ultimately became "SS Commando Battalion 502".[47]

The varying characters of the SS probation soldiers of the "Special Unit for Special Duties Friedenthal" sent to Valdagno were not Wurzian's only problem: some of the SS men couldn't even swim! Their devotion to duty also varied: while some remained ideologically committed to the National-Socialist regime and the SS religion of "Blood and Earth", there were also some who were just waiting for a favorable opportunity to desert.[48]

Unlike the SS group, the first detachment of navy men, which arrived in Vald-agno at the beginning of January 1944, consisted of 20 first-class sport swimmers. They were led by *Oberfähnrich* Fritz Kind. There were famous names among them, like Herbert Klein, who had broken swimming records before the war. After the war Klein was an extraordinarily successful swimmer, breaking world records and winning at the Olympics. The magazine *Der Spiegel* even featured him in a

Elements of "Sea Commando Battalion Brandenburg", including members of the Kriegsmarine, Abwehr, SS and paratroopers, assembled in the Piazza Dante in Valdagno in spring 1944.

cover story and bestowing on him a number of honorary sporting titles.[49] Other well-known swimmers were Heinz Bretschneider and Albert Lindner, two famous crawl swimmers, Karl-Heinz "Kuddl" Kayser and Werner Bullin, both outstanding breaststroke swimmers, and Rudi Ohrdorf, a swimmer from Magdeburg who set a world record in the 100-meter breaststroke. Other expert swimmers were Gerd Schmidt, Manfred Laskowski, Heinz Lehmann and Walter Ernst.

The navy was thorough in selecting its future "sea fighters" – at least as far as their physical constitution was concerned. They were, however, clearly less committed later, when it came to carrying out special missions. Some of the navy swimmer elite had previously been employed as members of a demonstration and competitive swimming unit, giving high-diving and racing displays to raise troop morale and attract volunteers to the navy. Many had hoped that being a member of this unit would allow them to see out the war without seeing combat, but now they had been ordered to a special formation with an uncertain future. Their unanimous comment to Wurzian was, "If you think that we want any part of your suicide unit, you're wrong."[50]

It took a great deal of convincing on Wurzian's part to even get the navy men to take part in the physical training. This would soon prove the key to success, for as Wurzian recalled, "they soon became enthusiastic about the sporting side of the affair. Training! Training! No one objected to that."[51] Only with the necessary physical training would they have a chance to return safely from a mission. This was Wurzian's constant credo: most of the training was designed to enable the commando to make a safe return. A mission was no suicide assignment, rather it was an operation planned and carried out to the last detail with a well-thought-out plan for returning home safely. Only later, when the navy men realized that success depended on every single man and that the missions represented a controllable danger provided they were properly trained and prepared, did they lose their bias against the missions and the number of volunteers from among the competitive swimmers go up.

The approximately 60 men who arrived in Valdagno in the first weeks of 1944 were joined by others in the months that followed, mainly volunteers from the navy's training flotillas. There was no shortage of volunteers from there, as production of conventional submarines, including the latest types, was lagging. Many of these newly-trained and highly-motivated young men found themselves waiting for a ship and joined the sea commando unit as a way to get to the front. Following a suitability test, ultimately only the most capable among them were selected and sent to the commando unit.[52] The volunteers included officers, NCOs and enlisted men. Every member of the unit swore to commit himself fully – not to self-sacrifice, but to employ his mental and physical abilities to the utmost.

Hand-to-hand combat training and jiu-jitsu were an important part of the combat diver training program.

Not unexpectedly, the different origins and ideologies of the various groups quickly led to an unhealthy competition between the navy, *Abwehr* and SS for control of the new unit. For this reason Wurzian has very unpleasant memories of the first few weeks in Valdagno. There were frequent disputes between the three branches of the armed services, for each was convinced that his unit would soon be placed in overall command of the sea commando battalion. Officially it was still under the command of *Hauptmann* Neitzert of the *Abwehr II*, but both the SS men and the sailors were convinced that this would soon change, and both groups displayed an air of self-confidence befitting their convictions. Unfortunately no clarifying order or decision was forthcoming from the OKW.

In February 1944 the commando unit's supply situation deteriorated even further. A conflict had obviously also broken out in Berlin over who was now responsible for the unit. The ill will within the unit reached a temporary climax when Wurzian announced no pay had been received from *Abwehr* headquarters in Berlin for some time and that deliveries of foodstuffs had also been further reduced. This affected Wolk's combat divers as well as the Germans.

Wolk and Wurzian discussed the situation, and according to Wurzian's account it was Wolk who came up with the idea of ambushing a partisan food depot and stealing the necessary supplies. Wolk did see a potential problem if Italian soldiers attacked the partisan camp, as this might cause anger among the populace, but Wurzian saw no other possibility but to select a number of personnel from his divided unit to carry out the attack. Wurzian ultimately came up with the solution of dressing the Italian soldiers in German uniforms. Commanded by Wolk, and using trucks loaned by the German air force in Valdagno, the surprise attack was carried out and brought the hoped-for booty in food and fuel.

Wurzian enjoyed the maximum possible freedom in designing the training program, but to a large degree he based it on the Italian methods. Elite sport was the only tie that bound together his extremely mixed unit. The combat divers were soon jokingly calling themselves the "Sports Club". Because of the wide variations in levels of training, future combat missions were not yet a topic in early 1944, and if they were discussed at all it was at the command level.

For the outside world, the combat diver commando was disguised as a military convalescent home where sports and physical activity were used to return the wounded to fighting trim. In fact, intensive sport made up the bulk of the daily routine. Herbert Klein later recalled the five main components:

"Our activities in Valdagno consisted of:

1. *Long-distance swimming.* Daily we swam around the indoor swimming pool for two to three hours in our rubber suits.

2. *Diving.* A simulated ship's hull had been placed in the swimming pool. There we practiced approaching the hull submerged and affixing a bomb about one meter long to the bilge keel beneath the water.

3. *Hand-to-hand combat.* It was important in the event that we would later have to leave the water in enemy territory after blowing up a ship and make our way to our own lines.

4. *Light athletics.* Designed to bring the frogman's irreplaceable weapon, his body, to its peak through sport.

5. *"Butter eating".* We were given extra rations, specially selected for us, to offset the great heat loss caused by the constant swimming."[53]

The swimming training in the indoor pool was expanded through practical exercises with the diving equipment: dives to five meters beneath the diving tower and exchange of diving equipment and masks, blowing water from the mask, weight exercises, distance and time diving, orientation dives at night and with blackened masks, dives into the water from the upper gallery with full equipment, and during, before and after: seemingly endless distance swimming on the back with full equipment – sometimes up to six hours at a time.

"The water must become your new habitat!" preached Wurzian, and he repeated the exercises until the future combat divers could do them in their sleep. This was in fact the only goal of these exercises before continuing their training in open water. Once there it would be impossible to correct errors, so they had to feel so comfortable in the water that they could immediately recognize and correct any danger or error.

There were many days when the combat divers had swim fins on their feet longer than boots or athletic shoes. Training was not limited to the swimming pool, however, as the men had to spend some time each day on the sports field. There were the regular morning calisthenics before breakfast, and after lunch there were other types of sport such as shot put, running and the broad jump. Senior Engineer Neumeyer dispatched an expert jumper and a judo instructor to Valdagno from Berlin. There was no target shooting, as combat divers did not carry pistols on their missions.

The future sea commandos underwent frequent medical checks and it was stressed that they must immediately report even the most minor physical weakness or complaint.

Sport filled their days and nights, and, as Wurzian later recalled, "they soon forgot that they had wanted no part of a 'suicide squad' and became enthusiastic participants."[54] With time the combat divers' physical fitness became so good they regretted being unable to display it publicly. There were frequent competitions in the various disciplines and records were even set. To provide some variety in the daily training routine, therefore, Wurzian allowed himself to be talked into a sports meet: a large, public swim meet took place in the Marzotto aquatic facility at the beginning of March. The event consisted of several freestyle swimming competitions and high diving from the dive tower, with the German and Italian participants striving to outdo one another. The program ended with a lively and exciting water handball match.[55]

The second public meet was held several weeks later on 30 April, a Sunday, and consisted of a soccer match between the Italian team from the Marzotto textile mill and a mixed team of German sea commandos and Italian combat divers. It quickly became apparent that the sea commandos were more at home in the water than on green grass, for they lost the game 6:2.

As entertaining as the soccer match had been, it brought Wurzian a severe reprimand from Berlin, for several days after the game the newspaper *Il popolo vicentino* had published a game report including the full names of the German participants. It named Adolf Wolschendorf, Karl König, Walter Wimmer, Walter Dyck, Richard Reimann, Malle, Karl-Heinz Kayser, Rudi Ohrdorf and Walter Ernst! As well, the names of the two Italian team members Giari and Ridolfi, both *Gamma* combat divers, were also printed. This was obviously a significant security breach and resulted in an order to enhance secrecy about the unit and its personnel.[56] Furthermore they were no longer permitted to leave the "military convalescent home" as a team, for their sporting performances threatened its veil of secrecy.

In March 1944 an *Abwehr* officer arrived in Valdagno who would play a significant role in the future of the detachment: *Hauptmann* Friedrich Hummel, the leading German practitioner in ship sabotage and one of the *Abwehr*'s best agents. Hummel's love of the sea had led him to serve aboard training vessels, sailing ships and steamers of the German merchant marine, which took him to almost every corner of the earth – to South America, Africa, Indonesia, China and Japan. For almost two years he was master of the *Passat*, an imposing four-masted bark, which survives to this day in Travemünde.

It was Hummel's goal to receive a master's ticket in the German merchant marine. In 1933, when the effects of the worldwide economic crisis were being increasingly felt in commercial shipping, he changed his plans and joined the police service in Altona. He began as a simple auxiliary policeman, but after two years he moved to the Secret State Police. In 1937 he successfully participated in the 4th Chief Inspector Candidate course at the Police Institute in Berlin-Charlottenburg. Scarcely five years after becoming a policeman, Hummel became a chief inspector and head of a police station in the port of Hamburg.

Further appointments followed, the last in 1944 to chief detective superintendent. This rapid rise can be attributed entirely to Hummel's personal and professional strengths.[57] In addition to his professional career, Hummel used his free time to attend classes at Hamburg University. It was not until 1941, however, that he was able to take his first state law exams, having been given leave from the armed services to do so.

The war initially interrupted his successful career as an active detective, as Hummel volunteered for the military.[58] In doing so he met a requirement set by his top superior, *SS-Obergruppenführer* Reinhard Heydrich, that each detective should prove himself at the front before being considered for senior positions in the SS and the police.

Hummel also demonstrated his capabilities as a *Wehrmacht* officer, ultimately winning the Knight's Cross. After a number of voluntary exercises with the anti-tank battalions and participation in the Polish Campaign, Hummel developed into an extremely daring officer, whose acumen and proficiency in foreign languages did not fail to capture the attention of the *Abwehr*. He was recruited by the military

Hauptmann Friedrich Hummel was one of the Abwehr's finest agents.

secret service and in autumn 1941 transferred to *Abwehr II* as a *Leutnant*. After the usual specialized training in sabotage and subversive fighting in Brandenburg, from November 1941 to February 1944 he served as group leader of the *Abwehr* war organization in Madrid, thanks to his proficiency in Spanish.

Hummel established a network of saboteurs during his time in Spain and these attacked installations in Gibraltar and British ships in Spanish ports, especially Cartagena.[59] To avoid diplomatic entanglements, Hummel was careful to leave no tracks that might suggest that the Germans were behind the attacks. The principal targets were British ships delivering oranges to Great Britain. With increasing frequency they also became carriers of explosive charges: Hummel's men secretly filled orange crates with explosives, which exploded on the high seas or in British ports during unloading. For this reason, the orange ships from Spain soon became the terror of British port authorities.[60] Eventually the port workers refused to unload ships coming from Spain until every load of oranges had been inspected for hidden explosives.

Hummel also carried out special missions on the mainland: with the help of Spanish workers he succeeded in smuggling a powerful time bomb into a tunnel in the Rock of Gibraltar where the British had their ammunition dump. The bomb was concealed in a light metal housing that was identical in shape to a British artillery shell. If the bomb had gone off it would have detonated thousands of large shells. The operation was foiled, however, when one of Hummel's men betrayed the plan to the British and the bomb was defused.[61]

Friedrich Hummel found another target for his saboteurs and bomb experts following the Italian surrender in late 1943: Italian ships in Spanish ports. Disguised as Spanish fishermen, Hummel and his saboteurs approached the Italian ships at night in rowboats and placed small charges which were at least capable of rendering the vessels unable to maneuver. The *Abwehr* proudly recorded the results of its subversive activities: approximately 40,000 GRT of Italian shipping had been immobilized. By his own account, Hummel personally sank 50,000 GRT of enemy shipping[62] and destroyed a large quantity of aircraft and fuel tanks awaiting transport.

Hummel's operations continued successfully until the beginning of 1944, when one of his sabotage groups made a fateful mistake. One moonless night in the port of Cartagena, *Abwehr* agent Carl Kampen left the German ship *Lipari* in a rowboat, together with ship's officers Walter Schröder and Hans Ritter, to attack the Italian tanker *Lavoro*. Kampen intended to place a mine on the tanker's outer hull, but he made a serious error while arming the fuse alongside the *Lavoro*. The result was a huge explosion, which killed the saboteur. The detonation capsized the rowboat, but the two officers were able to save themselves. They were taken prisoner and German responsibility for the sabotage operations was revealed.

In the course of the diplomatic complications that followed the "Kampen Affair", and under pressure from the Foreign Office, at the end of January 1944 Hummel was forced to halt his sabotage activities in Spanish ports. His next assignment was a secret commando operation against Allied supply lines in Algeria, with Hummel disguised as an Arab. Twice he succeeded in cutting important railway lines through acts of sabotage – in Tazah, an important junction between East and West Morocco, and in Ras el Aouin near Metlaoui (Tunisia). Hummel was subsequently transferred to the combat diver training detachment in Valdagno, where on 1 April 1944 he relieved its former commanding officer, *Hauptmann* Neitzert.

For security reasons, it was common practice for members of the *Abwehr* to use codenames. In Valdagno, therefore, *Hauptmann* Hummel became *Hauptmann* Hellmers. Through his vigor and outstanding leadership qualities, Hummel achieved in Valdagno what *Hauptmann* Neitzert had failed to fully accomplish: friction between the groups subsided and a common spirit slowly began to form. Hummel was an extremely competent commander. Both his subordinates and other offices in Valdagno regarded and accepted him as a competent commander. Wurzian later observed that Hummel "would have been the only one even capable of leading our wild bunch."[63]

Three teams were created to prevent the formation of groups from the various *Wehrmacht* elements and also to promote and expedite training. This move was intended to bring the men from the various service branches into a common order. By that time it had also become apparent that the navy was going to be given overall command of the sea commando battalion and that turf wars had become obsolete. The navy's new *Kleinkampfverband der Kriegsmarine*, or KdK (Navy Small Battle Unit) was officially established on 20 April 1944, and Rear Admiral Hellmuth Heye assumed overall command.[64] Of this Karl Dönitz later wrote: "When the responsibilities of the fleet headquarters were further reduced after the loss of *Scharnhorst* [on 26/12/1943, author's note], I finally tasked the former Fleet Headquarters chief-of-staff, Rear Admiral Heye, with the practical establishment of the small battle units. He successfully carried out this task as well as everything associated with assembling the material means and personnel necessary for the formation of the force. I smoothed all the roads for him organizationally. He was both operational commander and responsible officer in the Navy High Command for his operational mission. But in this special case it was necessary to proceed in this manner, in order to form a completely new combat unit with innovative combat methods during wartime. Veteran officers, mostly former submarine captains, were assigned to Admiral Heye as flotilla commanders. The personnel were all volunteers from every rank and branch of the navy, and from the end of 1944 a considerable number of them were young officers from the submarine arm."[65]

Admiral Heye recalled this period in his personal memoirs: "With the military situation in the winter of 1943-44, we were limited to the defensive at sea. It was common knowledge that for this reason I gave preference to many and small ships and other weapons in preference to larger units. Because of my views, therefore, Grand Admiral Dönitz thought me suitable for the task of creating innovative small battle units. *Korvettenkapitän* Frauenheim was assigned to me to assist in these beginnings, initially while I was still at fleet headquarters. I also added *Kapitän-leutnant der Reserve* Michael Opladen and soon afterwards *Korvettenkapitän* Hans Bartels to my staff, because I considered these two ideally suited to this task."[66]

In his autobiography, Otto Skorzeny described the proceedings as follows: "Building on the experience of the Italians, Admiral Heye and his staff developed new and effective special weapons in a few months. The basic idea was to redesign what was already available whenever possible. Everything had to proceed as quickly as possible, for we all knew that we no longer had much time to lose."[67]

By decree of the OKW, effective 15 April 1944 all regular and special units assigned to coastal defense were attached to the *Kriegsmarine*, including the *Brandenburg* Division, which had previously been directly attached to the *Abwehr*: " The operational groups for non-conventional operations of the OKW/*Abwehr Amt*, of the *Brandenburg* Division, which has been engaged in the preparation and use of non-conventional weapons, are to be gradually transferred to the *Kriegsmarine* (Naval Operations Department) with all military assets."[68]

As a result of this decree, specialized units of significance to the new small battle force were to be released from *Abwehr* "assets" and incorporated into the navy's small battle units. On 21 June 1944 the former "Sea Commando Battalion *Brandenburg*", now dubbed "Small Battle Unit Training Detachment 700", was officially placed into service. Elements of the "Coastal Commando Battalion *Brandenburg*", which specialized in amphibious landings, were also taken into the navy's small battle force.[69] Formed in February 1944, the coastal commando unit was equipped mainly with assault boats and landing craft. Its 4th Company was conceived as the first German small battle unit. The company was initially to be equipped with "Smallest Torpedo Carriers" (so-called "Schneider boats"), but then was gradually to receive "*Linse*" (Lentil) type demolition boats. Since summer 1943 it had been based in Sesto Calende on Lago Maggiore. The *Abwehr*'s sea commando and coastal commando battalions formed the germ cell and the foundation of the navy's small battle units.

Otto Skorzeny was expanding his area of influence as the reorganization of the combat diver units was taking place. Skorzeny initially viewed the naming of Hummel as the new commander of the combat divers as a tactical advantage over the navy and a lever with which he hoped to achieve full control of this special unit in the near future and exercise direct influence on it. The OKW decree had now removed any SS influence over the ex-Brandenburger combat diver *Brandenburg*, however this did not prevent Skorzeny from formulating certain demands.

In February 1944 *Sturmbannführer* Skorzeny had become director of the SS "Special Weapons" project, under which, for example, fell the V-1 rockets manned by suicide pilots. In his new position Skorzeny now also claimed a say in the new type of underwater warfare. At the beginning of March 1944 Skorzeny had inspected the various types of non-conventional weapons in Lübeck and discussed the subject with Admiral Heye. Skorzeny later described his meeting with Heye: "A small, nimble gentleman of about 50 years greeted me. The basic ideas set forth to me by the admiral, with whom I soon had a good working relationship, were convincing and excited me."[70] Elsewhere Skorzeny wrote of Heye: "He was a seaman in the best sense of the word and an imaginative tactician."[71]

Admiral Heye wanted to continue training members of the SS to be combat divers, for according to the previously-cited OKW order, "the development and testing of these non-conventional weapons, insofar as they are the same as or resemble the assets transferred to the navy, … [remain] the responsibility of the navy, or are to be carried out in cooperation with the navy."[72] This was subject to the division of responsibilities, however, which specified that while the navy was responsible for the coastal areas, all inland missions, meaning lakes and rivers, fell to the SS. Although in theory this division of responsibilities was actually quite clear, conflicts of interest, petty rivalries and power struggles led to frequent conflicts between the navy's small battle force and the SS.

The divers could only be taken so far in the swimming pool, and in spring 1944 the search began for a suitable sea training camp on the Adriatic coast, where they could train in open water. It was Eugen Wolk who found a small island within Venice's lagoon which would serve as training camp for the second part of the sea commando training. The sea training camp was set up on the small island of San Giorgio in Alga, about three kilometers south of Venice. In former times the roughly 15,000-square-meter island had been home to a Benedictine monastery and since the beginning of the 1900s it had served first as an Italian military prison and later as an ammunition depot. A high wall ran around the perimeter of the island, shielding it from the curious. Two small docks provided the only access to the island from the Vecchio di Fusina Canal.

In March five men under the command of *Oberfähnrich* Fritz Kind were sent to Alga as an advance guard to prepare the premises there. This proved to be extremely time-consuming as considerable renovation work was required: centuries earlier the church had fallen victim to fire and the rest of the buildings were in poor condition. The hygienic facilities were unbearable and completely inadequate.

The advance detachment had to remove entire wagon-loads of rubbish from the rooms. The entire building complex had to be overhauled from the ground up. As well, many of the things necessary to set up housekeeping – such as lockers, cleaning materials, bunks – were not present. The existing space was only suitable for about 40 men. As more soldiers were supposed to be stationed there, contracts were issued for the construction of three wooden barracks on the island – one of 32 meters, one of 24 meters and one of 16 meters – plus an air raid shelter. In the beginning there was not a single usable vehicle available with which to supply the island, which was extremely difficult anyway as everything needed to sustain the camp had to be brought in from far away.

San Giorgio in Alga was also made to look like a military convalescent home to the outside world. The island was very isolated, and the ferry between Fusina and the Lido passed within visual range only occasionally. But even the strictest secrecy was of little use, for Italian civilian workers were brought in, and the school's true character soon became apparent to them. By the end of May 1944 the sea commando detachment in Valdagno had reached a strength of about 80 men, and many candidates, having completed the five-month basic training course in the swimming pool, were ready to begin open water training. As the buildings on Alga were now ready for occupancy and the water temperature in the lagoon had risen, the navy training camp was officially placed into service at the same time as Training Detachment 700. The training camp on Alga was given the designation "Training Course Camp 701".[73] *Oberleutnant* Strenge was named camp commander. On 1 September he was replaced by *Leutnant* (Naval Artillery) Kummer. In mid-June the first group began relocating from Valdagno to Venice.

Because of the growing partisan threat in the Agno Valley, Alfred von Wurzian had no regrets about moving his base from Valdagno to Alga.[74] The true scope of the threat was revealed on Sunday, 11 June 1944: the Agno Valley was also a wonderful hiking area and touring the mountains was a pleasant sporting activity, consequently many of the German soldiers enjoyed spending their free Sundays taking long hikes and strolls in the area around Valdagno. During one such walk on this Sunday afternoon there was a tragic occurrence in the small village of Contrada Borga: four unarmed sea commandos were on their way back to Valdagno after hiking in the mountains when shots rang out. *Maat* Georges, an SS probation soldier, was hit and killed.

That same day the German garrison in Valdagno carried out a massive "retaliatory action". The operation, carried out by forces under *Leutnant* Stey of the 11th Special Purpose Air Signals Battalion, including the SS Special Operations Battalion, a unit with experience in anti-partisan warfare, turned into a bloodbath. The entire male population of Contrada Borga, 17 men altogether, were rounded up and killed with machine-guns and hand grenades. Then the village was burned to the ground. This drama, undoubtedly a war crime, was the prelude to further bloody battles between partisans and German troops in this region.[75]

On Monday, 12 June 1944, Wurzian and the headquarters of Training Detachment 700 moved from Valdagno to Alga for sea diving training. Part of Training Detachment 700 stayed in Valdagno and continued basic training under the direction of *Feldwebel* Ivo Haas of the *Abwehr*. This training camp subsequently bore the title "Training Course Camp 704". *Oberleutnant* (Naval) Herbert Völsch was named camp commander.

Coincident with construction of the training camp in Venice, in spring 1944 another base for the preliminary training of sea commandos had been built at the *SS-Junkerschule* in Bad Tölz. The SS school in Bad Tölz was the forge that produced the officer elite of the *Waffen-SS*, and it had a large, modern swimming facility with deep and shallow pools. Candidates would receive the same basic training as at Valdagno, prior to proceeding to Venice for sea training. The marine commando training course at Bad Tölz was officially placed in service on 1 July 1944 and was given the designation "Training Course Camp 702". In charge of the course was *Oberleutnant z.S.* Küsgen. The first course comprised 68 students.

List on the island of Sylt was selected as a second camp for open-water training. The List camp was designated "Training Course Camp 703", but it did not enter service until 1 November 1944. In the end it was used mainly as fall-back quarters when the training detachment lost its bases in Valdagno and Venice.[76]

With the transfer of the "Marine Commando Battalion *Brandenburg*" to the navy's commando unit as "Training Detachment 700", there was a change in command: at the end of June 1944 *Abwehr Hauptmann* Hummel reluctantly had to transfer command to an officer of the *Kriegsmarine*. On 21 June 1944 Navy Staff Doctor Armin Wandel assumed command of Training Detachment 700, the sea training camp in Venice and the two basic training schools in Valdagno and Bad Tölz. Wandel possessed valuable experience in diving medicine, and his position as a doctor was a welcome front for the battalion's "convalescent company" disguise.

Wandel had previously served as ship's doctor during two cruises into the South Atlantic on the U 129 in 1941. The navy's chief medical officer, Admiral Dr. Emil Greul, had had Wandel pulled out of the submarine medical service.[77] After his combat cruises Wandel initially took over the post of flotilla medical officer of the 26th Submarine Flotilla in Pillau and then the 11th Submarine Flotilla in Norway. Wandel served in Norway for almost two years, building up and expanding his flotilla hospital during that time.[78]

After two months as medical officer with the Operational Unit of Navy Group Command North in Heiligenhafen – which was responsible for preparatory measures for the training and first operations by the small battle force – in April 1944 Wandel was sent south on new duties. Initially he filled the post of medical officer attached to Operations and Training Headquarters South. This was the tactical command and operations headquarters for all small battle units stationed in Italy and was based in Sesto Calende on Lago Maggiore. Commander of the headquarters, whose units included Training Detachment 700, was *Leutnant* Schomburg. Wandel had already visited the two sea commando training camps in Valdagno and Venice during an inspection in early May 1944. He wrote in his medical diary: "In Valdagno I inspected a sea commando pre-school and its hygienic and sanitary facilities. The soldiers' quarters are located in a modern aquatic center, which is generously laid out and meets all requirements of an hygienic and sanitary nature. The quarters are roomy, airy and bright, the toilet facilities adequate and hygienic in every way. Kitchen facilities are modern and clean. The soldiers' state of health

Hauptmann Friedrich Hummel transfers command of Training Detachment 700 to Marinestabsarzt Dr. Armin Wandel on 21 June 1944 on Alga. Hummel and many of his men were anything but happy about this change in command.

is excellent, they are first-class specimens, all athletes. There were complaints, however, about frequent ear maladies such as inflammation of the middle ear, irritation of the middle ear and inflammation of the auditory canal as well as sinus infections, which are caused by diving."[79]

In mid-May 1944 at La Spezia, Wandel also met Count Borghese, commander of the *Decima Mas*, and his Italian *Gamma* divers. Back in Timmendorf, Wandel reported to Heye on this special unit and remarked that it would fit well into the small battle force and would be an asset to his unit. Admiral Heye thereupon appointed Wandel overall commander of the German navy combat divers. And so Wandel, contrary to the Geneva Convention which states that a doctor must not command a combat unit, became head of the newly-formed Training Detachment 700.[80]

Wandel, who with Heye and the *Kriegsmarine* at his back was now in a completely different position of power than Neitzert and Hummel had been with the declining *Abwehr*, was able within a short time to supply the two training camps in Valdagno and on Alga with the necessary installations and equipment.

Marinestabsarzt Dr. Armin Wandel with Rittmeister Erwein Graf von Thun-Hohenstein (center) and a Luftwaffe officer on the steps of the aquatic center in Valdagno. In the foreground is "Bonzo", Training Detachment 700's mascot.

Relay swimming in the big pool in Venice.

Also finally settled was the question of motor vehicles and fuel allocations for materials and rations procurement. Until the *Kriegsmarine* assumed command, the shortage of diving equipment was the main reason for the delayed open-water training. During negotiations with the main supplier in Milan, Wandel secured a promise that sufficient equipment for the safe conduct of regular training would soon be forthcoming.[81]

To introduce the new detachment to the various administrative centers in Venice, and to avoid the difficulties that inevitably arose in the procurement of the most necessary items by making personal contact with the various office heads, Wandel planned a major *Wehrmacht* display in swimming, diving and water polo for 2 July. It would be followed by a social evening with Italian entertainers on the island of Alga, to which all of the German and Italian office heads and Venetian honoraries would be invited. The display was open to the German armed services and the Italian public. For reasons of secrecy, the official organizer was *Oberstleutnant* Dr. Gehring, the local military commander in Venice. Training Detachment 700 was given the cover designation "Unit Wandel".

The races were held in the big swimming stadium at Venice's main railway station. The program consisted of: 100 m freestyle, 4 x 50 m breaststroke relay, trick diving, 4 x 50 freestyle relay, high diving, 100 m breaststroke, humorous interludes on the tower, medley relay, and finally a water polo match. The Venice departmental head donated prizes for the best swimmer, diver and water polo team. The event was very well received and two weeks later on a Sunday afternoon it was repeated in the swimming pool in Valdagno.

Wandel reciprocated for the administrative centers' support in expanding the training camp on Alga: for example, it turned out that, when it came to the recovery of torpedoes, the combat divers were much more effective than helmet divers. Beginning in mid-July, two combat divers were attached to the torpedo arsenal in Venice at all times to recover torpedoes test-fired by two-man attack boats. Helmet divers took much more time to recover torpedoes than combat divers and required greater supporting resources.

Wandel also hoped for more support for his new detachment from the SS, namely Otto Skorzeny, for the union of the *Abwehr* with the Central Security Office's security service was by then largely complete, and as a result Skorzeny had become even more influential. The process was begun by the "Führer Order of 12 February 1944", in which Hitler ordered the formation of a unified intelligence service under the command of the SS. The motivation for this reorganization, which the SS had long been calling for – and which Skorzeny described as "a long-prepared and secretly desired coup by Schellenberg" – was to be found in failed *Abwehr* sabotage operations in Spain and the desertion to the British intelligence service of a large number of *Abwehr* operatives in Turkey.[82]

On Hitler's orders, on 1 June 1944 the bulk of the *Amt Abwehr/Ausland* was attached to Office VI of the Central Security Office under the new title "Amt Mil" (General Staff *Oberst* Georg Hansen commanding) and thus came under the authority of the SS, solidifying its sole claim to espionage and sabotage. Within the *Amt Mil*, which also included the "*Regiment Kurfürst*", there was Office *Mil-D* (under General Staff *Major* Naumann), in which all sabotage-technical installations of the former *Abwehr* and the associated personnel of *Abwehr II* were brought together. *Mil-D* was subordinated to Otto Skorzeny, who thus gained an extensive area of influence. From then on Skorzeny's commando force was responsible for those commando operations that had previously been reserved largely for the "*Branden-burgers*". At the end of June 1944, following a meeting with Mussolini at Garda Lake, Skorzeny took the opportunity to visit the two training camps in Valdagno and Venice. He arrived in Valdagno on 30 June, inspected the buildings and even made a practice dive in the pool. He wrote: "I never would have expected to find such a large indoor swimming pool in such a small town. My men watched my first attempts with the breathing apparatus with great enjoyment. As I had long been a water rat, I was able to emerge from the affair without embarrassing myself."[83]

Opposite
Top: *At the end of June 1944 Sturmbannführer Otto Skorzeny (right) visited the two combat diver training centers in Valdagno and on Alga. Here he is seen during the boat ride to Alga with Marinestabsarzt Dr. Wandel. Bottom: In San Giorgio harbor, Wandel describes the architectural features of the island.*

Above: Otto Skorzeny in bathing trunks as he prepares to don diving equipment in preparation for a dive in Venice Lagoon.

As he was on a tight schedule, Skorzeny went on to Venice the same day and there repeated the practice dive in the lagoon off Alga. Wandel, who accompanied Skorzeny all day, asked him if the SS might provide him with 25 Russian prisoners of war to help run the ground organization on the island (procurement of rations, housecleaning, mess duties, routine traffic, boat duty, procurement of supplies) and to operate the anti-aircraft guns recently installed there. Skorzeny said that he would, but in spite of repeated follow-up inquiries by Wandel the Russian forced laborers never arrived in Venice, and consequently the men taking part in the course had to carry out all the other duties in addition to their training. This of course seriously delayed the training.

At the beginning of July 1944 Skorzeny sent the ambitious *SS-Untersturmführer* Walter Schreiber to Valdagno.[84] Schreiber came from an Austrian civil service family and had completed elite National-Socialist training. After attending several prestigious traditional schools he switched to the National Political School (NA-POLA) in Vienna. He subsequently enrolled in the University of Vienna in the faculty of Law and Political Science. While attending school he was a member of the *Jungvolk* and the Hitler Youth. On his 18th birthday, the earliest possible opportunity, the eager law student Schreiber volunteered for the *Waffen-SS* and joined the National-Socialist party. He saw combat with various SS armored units. His role in the famous tank battle at Kharkov and other actions attracted the attention of his superiors and promotion was rapid. Decorated with the Iron Cross, Second Class, the Tank Battle Badge in Silver and the Wound Badge in Black, in early 1944 he attended a special course for SS tank NCOs to prepare him for entrance into the officer ranks. In the final course report, Schreiber's character was assessed as follows: "Above average mentally, nimble-minded and keen."[85] As a newly-promoted *SS-Untersturmführer*, Schreiber, who was also an excellent athlete and had made a request to the SS personnel office for a special mission abroad, joined the SS Special Detachment of the RSHA Dept. VI-S. In Valdagno Schreiber was to act as Skorzeny's official representative and as liaison officer between the navy and SS members in Training Detachment 700. Simultaneously Schreiber began combat diver training so that he could also participate in operations himself.

CHAPTER EIGHT

SEA TRAINING IN SAN GIORGIO ON ALGA

While Training Detachment 700 consisted of just about 80 men when Wandel took over, during the summer new arrivals caused its strength to increase rapidly to 280 men. By the end of August there were already 170 men stationed on Alga (about 130 Germans and 40 Italians), which represented the limit at that time. Further barracks were required to accommodate additional personnel. And yet the shortage of space on Alga continued. At the end of August, therefore, a transit camp was built in Limena near Padova for combat divers who had completed their training and those returning from operations. A stores facility for diving equipment not immediately required for operations or training was also set up in Limena. At the beginning of September a second fall-back camp was established on the Lido. The commander of the local military post made available to Training Detachment 700 a wing of a local hotel which could accommodate about 40 men.

Not until the establishment of Training Detachment 700 under the *Kriegsmarine* and the move to Venice did Wurzian's work become somewhat simpler and more regular. He now had a somewhat clearer idea as to who his contacts in the *Wehrmacht* command were and where he should turn when he required materials or support. The earlier power struggles had subsided. Whereas he had formerly been responsible for just about everything, something of a "troubleshooter" in the mold of a company sergeant, now he was gradually able to fall back on the navy's support structure.

Wurzian came up with simple methods to allow the unit to grow even further: inside the monastery there were bedrooms which could accommodate four persons each. Wurzian arranged it so that the bedrooms had a mixed occupancy which cut right across the branches and ranks of the *Wehrmacht*. Italians and Germans also lived together in the quarters. Officers and men took all their meals together.

Initially there were still conflicts, for example one member of the SS refused to take orders from a naval officer. The unrest within the unit abated with time, however, and the walls were slowly broken down. Living and working together on a daily basis gradually caused an atmosphere of trust to grow within the group, soon resembling a true team spirit.

Every man on Alga had his own equipment. It consisted of a white knit wool suit, a pair of rubber pants, rubber jacket, diving equipment with clear mask, head camouflage cloth, fins, wristwatch, wrist compass, knife and pistol. Nose clamps, which were designed to prevent water from entering the nose, had been done away with while the unit was still in Valdagno. It was found that they were easily knocked off while working underwater. In the initial confusion that followed, the man usually surfaced. If this happened during an operation, it would usually result in his detection.

In Valdagno the Germans had been separated from the Italians during training and in quarters, but on Alga this barrier also disappeared. While there had been

Regardless of rank or nationality, all combat divers ate together in San Giorgio's large dining hall, which had once been a church.

many built-in safety measures in place during training in the pool at Valdagno, it soon became apparent that mutual assistance and trust were absolutely basic requirements during sea training, for during their practice missions Wurzian pushed the combat divers to the very limits of their physical and mental capabilities. In the beginning on Alga, the "close-knit team" desired by Admiral Heye became a community of shared suffering.

At Alga Wurzian tried to find practice missions for the combat divers that were as offensive and dangerous as possible. His goal was to make 90% of all conceivable dangers manageable through ceaseless training. The remaining 10% would have to be mastered by courage, confidence and luck.

Right in front of the former church there was a small boat dock, and this was the starting point for every practice mission. The canals and the Italian navy arsenal in Venice comprised the main training area. When the combat divers had reached a certain level of training, Wurzian would send them to the arsenal to steal something. One popular mission was to take a rowboat from the naval arsenal in Venice or a motor torpedo boat from the Canale Grande. Both were in fact completed successfully. These were practice missions which came very close to a real combat situation.

Swimming 10 kilometers in fins was a daily routine in Alga. The training plan also included an activity which might sound strange today: the "underwater shout". In the course of his expeditions, Hans Hass had discovered that attacking sharks could be put to flight by shouting at them underwater. That was the reason why Wurzian had his students practice this trick on their first day of sea training. Even if the combat divers never had to employ the underwater shout, its proven protection did have a calming effect.

Wurzian made sure that every training mission incorporated a certain "fun factor", in order to keep the men's spirits up. An example of this was the ambushing of a harbor master. One of the exercises regularly assigned by Wurzian called for the men to steal a crate of apples or tomatoes from the fruit market in Venice undetected and then transport it back to Alga under water. The farmers eventually realized they had been robbed, but were never able to find the thieves. They were unaware that it had been divers who had stolen their crates unnoticed. The angry farmers finally turned to Commander Dr. Köhn, military commander of the city and harbor, who was responsible not just for the harbor but the entire city of Venice. Dr. Köhn of course knew about the secret detachment on Alga and that the perpetrators of the thefts were to be found there. He told the farmers nothing, but did pass their complaints on to Alga and, when the "practice thefts" were not stopped, also to higher offices.

Alfred von Wurzian later recalled the summer months on Alga: "In the shadow of the Bridge of Sighs, over which the condemned once had to make their final walk, began a ghostly activity. Soon Venice really did believe in ghosts. Boats were secretly released from their anchorages with fishermen sleeping inside. When the fisherman awoke at dawn, he found his boat far from shore. He checked the anchor – but it was lodged firmly in the muddy bottom. … Unbelievable … Every night fruit disappeared from the barges tied up at the fruit market. The merchants placed guards, but next morning the baskets were half empty again. The Venice arsenal was closely guarded, nevertheless ghostly figures crept around the buildings and disappeared into the water. More guards were added, but it made no difference. One night a white hand reached over the edge of a gondola. There was no one to be seen and no sound to be heard. The couple in the boat froze in mid kiss and the horrified gondolier fell into the water. … It was just a tired diver who wanted to rest a little. Some believed it was ghosts, others enemy saboteurs. Apart from the city commandant no one knew about us, but he had to remain silent as our detachment was top secret. The stack of files on his desk grew higher every day. Venice had become unsettled. Every night shots rang out over the lagoon. The nervous sentries challenged every oil slick, every piece of driftwood in the water, then fired

This engine-driven pump made it possible to quickly fill the tanks with up to 200 bar of oxygen.

at it. The uproar did not stop. The city commandant at first adopted a fatherly tone and then pleaded for the mischief to stop, but such an ideal opportunity to practice for the real thing could not be had anywhere else. Finally the man became furious and filed official complaints."[86]

Wurzian had no intention of abandoning his target object, especially as it brought additional rations to Alga. He therefore decided to send the harbor commander a message in order to silence him: Wurzian ordered a practice mission into the commandant's office. The six combat divers selected for the exercise had to swim from Alga through the canals to Venice and enter the office unseen. On the commandant's desk they left a small box, which was ticking suspiciously, and a small card "…with best wishes from the canal pirates". The entire raid took only a few minutes, and in no time the divers disappeared back into the canal without being seen. The commandant was more than a little shocked when he arrived for work and found the box on his desk, and he was forced to endure an agonizing wait until a fireman arrived to "disarm" the time bomb. When the box was opened, the suspected time bomb turned out to be his own large alarm clock, which had inexplicably disappeared from his bedside table that night. After this experience the harbor commandant was much easier to get along with and open to all the wishes of the combat divers.

Wurzian always impressed upon his men not to allow themselves to be caught while on practice missions, for they might be shot or taken prisoner. All exercises were conducted under realistic conditions. Practice missions by long-distance swimmers were carried out almost every night, for only night missions could be considered for the real thing. Groups of ten combat divers were taken by boat out into the Adriatic and dropped off somewhere at midnight. Each man had to find his own way back to the island using his wrist compass. No communication between divers was permitted at sea. The first would arrive back on Alga at six in the morning, the last not until noon. Much more difficult was the bottom walk: with lead shoes on their feet, lead weights on their belly belts, Belloni suit and bulky breathing apparatus, the combat divers had to advance at depths of up to forty meters, often against currents with speeds of four meters per second. They struggled against it, leaning forward more than 45 degrees. Mud and underwater sandstorms shrouded them. Each pair of divers was joined by a hand line, and using their compasses they had to find an object previously placed on the bottom and retrieve it.

The tanker *Tampico*, lying not far off the island, and the steamer, *Iliria*, at anchor about two kilometers away, served as practical training objects for diving under a ship's hull. The *Tampico* was 20 meters broad and had a draft of about five meters. The combat divers practiced approaching silently and attaching their bombs to the keel with screw clamps. Wurzian made an interesting observation

Fresh lime, which absorbed exhaled carbon dioxide, is poured into the breathing bag.

Eight men row the cutter to the Tampico, where training exercises took place. Manning the rudder is Alfred von Wurzian.

Friedrich Hummel and Alfred von Wurzian prepare for a dive. Both are wearing the Belloni dive suit.

during this exercise: as long as the divers had the clear surface above them they were calm, but when they went under the tanker and felt the hull of the ship above them, blocking their direct route to the surface, they became tense, and at some point, after the fifth or sixth time, they exhibited clear signs of panic.

He later described this experience as follows: "Earlier, in Valdagno, I had selected four exceptionally capable divers to assist me in my teaching activities. One bright day I carried out the first practice dive with them in the Venice lagoon. The object was to dive under one side of the tanker and surface on the other. While escorting the first two divers down, however, I immediately noticed that the cloudiness of the water and the feeling of having an indeterminate depth below were making the two divers uneasy. So I attached a line to their diving equipment and held the two ends in my hands. But then came a new surprise. Instead of passing straight under the ship, they moved away in the direction of the stern. I seized the lines and led the two under the hull of the ship. Slowly we went deeper and deeper.

It became ever darker. The pair hovered before me like ghostly shadows in the murky water. The ship's hull loomed over us like an overwhelming dome. Suddenly I noticed that one of the divers was beginning to breathe spasmodically. He tried to rip the mouthpiece of the oxygen device from his mouth. That would have meant certain death for him, for it is unlikely that I could have got the man, who was already flailing wildly, back to the surface. So I gave him a hard smack on the back with the flat of my hand and swam around until he could see me. He immediately calmed down. We were able to continue on our way – beneath the ship's keel and back to the surface. Later, when I asked the man why he had become uncertain, he told me that he couldn't give me a reason. He had suddenly had the feeling that he was hopelessly trapped beneath the ship. The hull hovering above him had such a terribly oppressive effect on him that he felt that he must suffocate."[87]

Panic reactions such as this were the most frequent cause of accidents under water. Clear thinking was overwhelmed by primeval survival instincts which were

Wurzian and comrades after a dive. They are in the cutter which will take them back to Alga from the Tampico. Fatigue is visible on their faces.

almost impossible to counteract. Flight to the surface seemed the only way out. And if the direct route to the surface was blocked – by a ship's hull or a cave roof – then the spiral of panic turned even faster. Wurzian knew about this natural reaction and he pushed every single diver's training until he reached the point of panic. In Wurzian's eyes a combat diver was not mentally prepared for actual combat missions until he had experienced the signs of approaching panic in his own body. "I took every single man in turn, dove under the ship with him and each time stayed for up to 20 minutes in the gloomy depths directly beneath the ship. That was good, for it soon became clear that each diver had to go through a nervous crisis. Some did not encounter it until their third or fourth diving attempt, but they all had to put it behind them," recalled Wurzian.[88]

Wurzian took part in every one of these practice dives beneath the *Tampico*, and he was soon making a dozen or more dives per day. The stress on Wurzian of course became noticeable, and there came a time when he noticed a brief period of dizziness and felt his head swimming before each dive and then for two or three minutes felt on the verge of passing out – typical early signs of oxygen poisoning. Other symptoms included sleep interruptions and buzzing in the ears.

Wurzian remembered: "Soon I felt at the end of my tether. I saw stars before my eyes every time I dived. When I returned to the surface I was unconscious for a few seconds. But I couldn't allow my students to notice, otherwise the feeling of security they had gained so slowly would have lost for good."[89] When Wurzian felt himself becoming dizzy while surfacing, he allowed a larger quantity of oxygen to flow into the breathing bag, which carried him to the surface and bore him safely there. And during the interval when one trainee was climbing onto the *Tampico* and another entering the water, he drifted on the surface half deaf with his face mask pulled down, regaining his strength until he was ready to dive again. Wurzian had been involved in a serious diving accident during the expeditions with Hans Hass, which had lingering effects. These additional weeks of destruction of his health through hours of hyperbaric oxygen breathing now did further damage to his health and were unfortunately to have even more negative effects later.

Wurzian's training exercises, which were designed to push every man to the limits of his abilities, resulted in two fatal accidents: Administrative Petty Officer and master swimmer Werner Bullin was lost on 20 June 1944 and it was eight days before his body could be recovered. The probable cause was a blockage in the oxygen line, which caused him to lose consciousness and drown. The second fatal accident occurred on 31 August 1944. During a practice dive, paratrooper *Obergefreiter* Herbert Klamt became faint, vomited into his diving equipment and suffocated. He was buried in Venice's cemetery on San Michele on 5 September.

The sportsmen, who were just beginning to feel confident diving in open water, were stunned by these unforeseen accidents. Wurzian recalled: "We had all received a shock. The sporting aspect of our work had blinded us to its dangerous nature. Personally I have never believed that it is possible to convince the majority of people that a hero's death is something worth striving for. Certainly I was not. But I was convinced that our work was not excessively risky if the divers were well-trained."[90]

The training activities soon returned to their familiar routine, however. Wurzian later wrote: "After a time the adventurous appeal of our missions and the feeling of being able to accomplish something on one's own gained the upper hand. The old cheerful relationship between comrades was soon restored."[91]

After the two accidents detachment commander Wandel planned to install a special rescue device on the diving equipment. An air bag was to be attached to the oxygen tank next to the breathing bag. It went round the neck like a ruff and could be filled with oxygen from the tank by pulling an emergency cord. An overpressure valve was to be fitted to the "ruff" to allow the diver to release pressure and prevent the slowly rising pressure from bursting it. The system brought the diver to the surface and once there the "ruff" kept his head above water. This prevented drowning and made the diver easier to locate. At this late stage in the war, however, German industry was incapable of putting the plan into practice; but Wandel's idea does show very clearly that employment of the German naval commando force was anything but a planned suicide mission. The safe return of every combat diver and a high operational safety factor were both priorities.

In mid-July 1944 Senior Engineer Neumeyer, together with *SS-Hauptsturmführer* Gerhardt and a *Herr* Enzmann of the German explosives firm WASAG, visited Venice to conduct experiments with the newly-developed explosives and explosives packets.[92] At that time, WASAG's production program was essentially limited to the manufacture of technical explosives, detonators, shotgun cartridges, celluloid, glycerin and sulfuric acid.

The explosives trials conducted on an old steamer provided by the harbor commandant proved very successful, and Neumeyer promised delivery of the first 70 explosive packets with the newly-developed "Nipolit" high explosive by the beginning of August. The new explosive packets had a special filling which combined nitrocellulose, nitroglycerine or diethylendiglycol, and nitropenta. Their explosive power was many times greater than the Italian explosive packets, which were filled with TNT. The new charges weighed 7.5 kg and had to be pulled through the water by the diver.

As encouraging as the effectiveness of the new explosive charges was, another factor restricted the employment of the combat divers: for what was now lacking

Funeral for Obergefreite Herbert Klamt, killed in a diving accident off Alga. A mixed German-Italian honor guard accompanied the casket from Alga to the Venice cemetery on the island of San Michele.

was the heart of the explosive charge – the clockwork detonator produced by the Italians. This shortage was relieved at the end of July, when 50 clockwork fuses were received from the Borletti firm of Milan. These later proved almost unusable, however, as sabotage made the clockwork mechanisms unreliable.

After a brief familiarization period on Alga, the daily routine normalized very quickly. On 30 July Wandel was able to note in his war diary: "The training of the navy detachment – sea commandos is being pursued most energetically, in part at the cost of the internal running of the camp. It comprises work with the Belloni suit under the ship by day and night, fin swimming with and without suits, work with the small diving equipment, swimming with explosive charges, compass swimming and simulated combat missions." By tightening up the training and, more importantly, through the delivery of sufficient diving equipment, it was possible to reduce the training time for combat divers in open water from four to two months.[93]

Wandel personally took part in the sea commando training: "During my two months as detachment commander and my activities as Training Detachment 700's medical officer, in addition to my duties I have been able to pursue my dive

On the deck of the Tampico, detachment commander Dr. Wandel observes tests with a newly developed underwater explosive. Clearly visible are the screw clamps used to attach the explosive packets to the bilge keel.

training to the extent that I hope to be able to report completion of my training as a sea commando before the end of this training period. During a night exercise on 3 August, I was able to demonstrate to the men that, even without training, I, the detachment commander, can successfully complete a major exercise with distance swimming and approach to a tanker under combat conditions in operational gear, and in doing so perform better than some others who are much farther ahead in their training."[94]

Wurzian quickly became Wandel's right hand, and Wandel turned to him for advice on many questions, both with regard to training and operations. Just four weeks after taking command, Wandel recommended Wurzian for promotion to officer. The recommendation was accompanied by an evaluation of *Oberfähnrich* Wurzian dated 26 July 1944, which read in part: "The *Oberfähnrich* is of average height, slim, with a fresh, open nature, well turned out with a military bearing and appearance. Physically very fit. Athlete. Lively, well-liked comrade. Mentally active, lively conversationalist. Strong personality, knows how to present his views. Committed to duty, enjoys his work because of interest in his duties. Willingly accepts responsibility and possesses decision-making ability. Independent in action and quick to take advantage of opportunities. Knows how to back up his position, has grasp and is a capable organizer. Many interests, inclined towards positive criticism. Knows how to deal correctly with subordinates, get the job done, possesses their full respect. Commits himself fully and successfully to his duties. A good example ideologically. Performed magnificently during formation of a special detachment and in every way meets the qualifications for an officer. *Oberfähnrich* von Wurzian was recommended for the Iron Cross, First Class. He promises to become an above-average officer."[95]

In his letter to the Replacement and Training H.Q. South, Wandel commented that Wurzian "is hampered by his assignment to the navy and under normal conditions should have become an officer a long time ago. Like Wurzian, all the others from the *Abwehr*, some of them the most excellent chaps, have been overlooked in promotion."[96]

Without completing officer school, Alfred von Wurzian was promoted to the rank of Lieutenant of the Naval Artillery retroactive to 1 April 1944. With it came the job of liaison man between Training Detachment 700 and Navy Special Staff attached to the Italy Staff of the Reich Minister for Armaments and War Production under Commander Carl-Siegfried Ritter von Georg, which required Wurzian to make several trips to Como and Milan. Disciplinarily, Wurzian remained part of the Regiment *Kurfürst*, even though from autumn 1944 this was attached to the Reich Central Security Office as part of the creation of a unified secret service. This double subordination of Wurzian's is a good example of the confused structure that existed after the disbandment of the *Abwehr*: for the purposes of discipline and service membership he was still – like all members of the *Amt Mil* – subordinate to the armed services, even though organizationally the *Amt Mil* had been incorporated into Department VI of the Reich Central Security Office, the SS, and was technically supposed to be under its direction.[97] In practice, however, Wurzian served for the *Kriegsmarine* and as a Lieutenant of the Naval Artillery wore a navy rank!

After the initial difficulties and uncertainties associated with the initial and sea training, the methods had been tested and refined, and this was clearly reflected in the state of training of the combat divers. In mid-August Wandel and Wurzian together inspected the preliminary school in Bad Tölz, and Wandel commented on the state of training in his war diary: "The state of training is good, exceeding expectations. Disciplinarily, the course makes a good impression; the men are eager and approach their duties with enthusiasm. The SS and navy are on the best of terms. The commander of the SS officer school praised the course's excellent military bearing and held up his men as examples. The instructors sent to Bad Tölz have performed extremely well and are the main reason why the course's state of training is this high."[98]

The entire course in Bad Tölz comprised 118 men, whereas a training unit usually consisted of 20 naval personnel. For reasons of secrecy, training was usually conducted at night between 2200 and 0600 hours. The first group of 22 men was sent from Bad Tölz to Venice at the end of August, their swimming pool training having taken seven weeks. As there were only a few combat divers in Valdagno at that time, another 29 men were sent there from Bad Tölz. A few days later, after the course participants had mustered in Valdagno, Wandel wrote in his diary: "It can be stated that the state of training is significantly higher compared to previous courses, which can be attributed in part to the experience gained during training and also to a strict conduct of the training process. The men are enthusiastic about their task, morale is good, their desire is to come to grips with the enemy as soon as possible. Most of the men were sent to Italy without weapons and some without tropical uniforms, which places a burden on the training camp. The required quantities of firearms and tropical uniforms are extremely difficult to procure in northern Italy. At the outset tests of courage were used to check the men's energy, strength of will and ability to overcome their fears. None of these tests, which included a headfirst dive from the 5-meter diving board, posed a threat to the lives or health of the men. Actively increasing the combat divers' energy, strength of will and ability to overcome fear was a vital factor in the combat effectiveness of the sea commandos. Any soldier who displayed shortcomings in this area was released as unsuitable with a clear judgment by the entire course about the man, who within the circle of sea commandos had failed to earn the right to call himself a combat

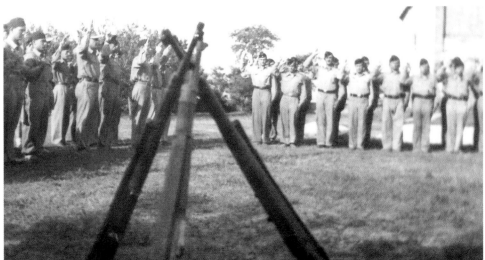

On 27 August 1944 all members of LK 700 took an oath of secrecy, as ordered by Headquarters, Small Battle Units. This took the form of a public oath-taking ceremony with subsequent party.

diver. A precondition for all tests of courage was the ability to swim and no physical handicaps. The relationship between Italians and Germans at the school [Alga: author's note] was tense. The Italians were jealous of our success in training and they conducted their training apart from us. With respect to this, it must be said that we surpassed the Italians in every respect in sea training and that we no longer learned from them, rather they from us!"[99]

During the first weeks in Venice Wurzian worked on further developing his attack methods. In the beginning, the tactic for attacking an enemy ship looked like this: when the combat diver got to within about 200 meters of the enemy ship, he ceased all movement. Suspended vertically in the water, he allowed the current to carry him to the ship, with only his camouflage-net-covered head out of the water. Tiny fin movements kept the diver on the surface and corrected direction. On reaching the hull, he drifted slowly with the current to roughly the midpoint of the ship and then silently submerged, exhaling calmly and almost completely. The loss of buoyancy was sufficient to cause him to submerge slowly. At a depth of several meters he placed the mouthpiece in his mouth, opened the breathing tube and continued breathing through the breathing apparatus. The diver had to be deep enough so that the opening of the oxygen bottle and subsequent inflation of the breathing bag did not pull him back to the surface. He also had to take care that clearing the water-filled mouthpiece did not cause suspicious air bubbles to rise to the surface. This meant that it was better to wait until he was under the keel to clear the mouthpiece and open the bottle. The explosive charges were attached to the keel using screw clamps and after the time detonator was set he began his egress. At some distance from the ship the diver surfaced, orientated himself using markers on the shore or swam back using his wrist compass. If conditions forced him to surface near the ship, he first inhaled all the air from the breathing bag, very cautiously expelled it beneath the keel and retained only enough in his lungs to easily allow him to reach the surface. If he failed to do this, the inflated air bag would carry him swiftly to the surface, where he would probably be spotted by an alert sentry.

It soon became apparent that this procedure demanded from every combat diver a high degree of discipline and steely nerves. The approach required additional concentration if searchlights were scanning the area around the ship. Despite intensive training, an emergency dive might result in mishandling of the diving equipment. This could cause the diver to swallow water, forcing him to cough and preventing him from submerging quickly.

Combat diver Herbert Klein remembered this risky method: "The dive was always a risky business: one had to exhale deeply in order to submerge silently by the side of the ship. Less buoyant, the body slid downwards, two, three, four, five, six meters deep, until it was beneath the ship's bilge keel. The water pressure and the need to breathe were tremendous, but the diver could not place the breathing tube in his mouth until he was under the bilge keel. The actual work of attaching the bomb with time-delay fuse to the bilge keel began. And then after this work there was always the swim back to land or to a boat that was sometimes waiting for the frogman kilometers away."[100]

Because of these risks and difficulties, in the summer of 1944 Wurzian revised the attack procedure to allow the diver to submerge farther away from the objective: about 200 meters from the target the combat diver took the breathing apparatus mouthpiece in his mouth, tightened his face mask if required, emptied the breathing bag and let himself sink feet-first to a depth of several meters below the surface. Then fresh oxygen was allowed to flow into the breathing bag, and with compass and depth gauge in front of his eyes the diver steered toward the objective, remaining as motionless as possible and using the current. After attaching the explosives to the ship's hull he allowed himself to drift onwards with the current, first surfacing at a safe distance from the ship. Then, swimming on his back, he began the journey back to his starting point.

In his diary Wandel described the advantages of Wurzian's new method as follows:

"1. Using the new method, the diver makes his approach to the target object from a distance of roughly 100 to 200 meters. This only requires him to break the surface briefly several times, thus the danger of being seen is much less compared to the other method.

2. The risk of swallowing water resulting in a strong urge to cough (old method) is gone with the new method, as the man has already switched the equipment to oxygen breathing prior to the last 100 to 200 meters from the target.

3. The new approach method allows the diver to move more rapidly without increasing the danger of being seen.

4. While approaching an enemy ship, fear of enemy searchlights or sentries with flashlights causes the sea commando to experience unbelievably high levels of mental stress, consequently the threat of a diver "cracking up" inside the enemy harbor and possibly mishandling the equipment when switching to oxygen is very real using the old method. The new method, however, has the advantage that the swimmer is already breathing oxygen during the last 100 to 200 meters and can thus submerge immediately at any time without having to first switch to oxygen."[101]

As much as the divers initially liked Alga, the longer they stayed the more confining the small island became. The measures to keep the unit secret meant a strict ban on passes and the avoidance of anything that might draw attention to the island or the activities of the soldiers. The first signs of "island madness" became apparent after several weeks on Alga. Disputes began breaking out over nothing, and when time permitted, everyone sought a small quiet corner where he could be alone at least for a little while. When Wurzian noticed these signs he approached Admiral Heye with a request to ease the restrictions on passes at least once a week and allow the men to go into prescribed areas of Venice for four hours on Saturdays. Heye, who had a high degree of trust in Wurzian, approved this relaxation and it contributed to a gradual improvement in morale. As Sundays were usually off-duty days, Saturday night was the only time when the men could be permitted to drink alcohol.

In mid-September there was an important change for the preliminary school in Valdagno: as some of the divers stationed there could not do their sea training in Venice because of rapidly cooling weather, field and infantry training were added to the curriculum for the first time. Preliminary training also had to be curtailed as the Marzotto factory was unable to heat the aquatic center because of a coal

Hummel, Wurzian and other comrades enjoy an ice cream sundae in Venice's St. Marcus Square on a Saturday afternoon in the summer of 1944.

shortage. The lost combat diver training was thus replaced with infantry training. A period of bad weather at the end of September, which caused the sea water to cool significantly, along with rough seas, also hampered training by Training Detachment 700. Moreover the unpredictable Bora, a cold, strong, gusty wind, had begun in the area of the northern Adriatic. In spite of this, Wandel hoped to be able to complete training of another 40 to 50 combat divers by the onset of winter.

September also marked the break between the navy and the SS and the end of combined combat diver training.[102] Over time there had been repeated disciplinary problems with detached SS members, who refused to acknowledge the navy's authority because they were under Otto Skorzeny's direct command. He retained the right to punish offences by his soldiers personally – an impossible situation for the commander of a military unit against which Wandel protested as soon as he took over. As early as 22 July he wrote in his war diary: "Most of the soldiers sent to Training Detachment 700 from SS Special Detachment 'Oranienburg' have been ordered here to prove themselves. There are always shirkers among them who negatively influence the training."[103]

At the end of August another group of SS men with their SS commander and liaison officer *Untersturmführer* Schreiber were sent to Venice for combat diver training, raising the total number of SS men in Valdagno and Alga to about 40. The swimming abilities of this second group of SS men were also substandard. After inspecting the group Wandel wrote in his diary: "The SS men were put through a brief diving and swimming exercise, during which one was eliminated from sea training. The average standard is not good, as many lack the necessary familiarity with and confidence in the water."[104]

The SS men were a constant source of unrest in the detachment. The final break between the navy and the SS probably had its origins in an incident which took place in Valdagno on 22 July: the murder of Rockstroh, a member of the SS sent to Italy for combat diver training. He had developed a plan to rob the civilians, mainly women and their children, taking shelter in the villas around Valdagno to escape the bombing of Verona. As he was hesitant to commit these robberies alone, he sought out an SS accomplice to accompany him; however, the man betrayed Rockstroh's plans to Wandel, who on 20 July had him arrested in preparation for sending him to Skorzeny for sentencing. To prevent his escape, Wandel posted two guards outside his cell. Then, during the night of 21-22 July Rockstroh was shot twice in the head and killed. The initial story was that he had been shot "by the arrest guards while attempting to escape".

Wandel, suspecting nothing, initially believed this version of events. Then, in mid-September, a Catholic priest from Valdagno came to see him on Alga. A woman from his parish had begun a relationship with a member of the training detachment with predictable consequences. The priest told Wandel that the soldier had told the pregnant woman that he could not marry her while the war was still going on, as he was an SS man and marriage to a non-German woman was out of the question. He wanted to marry her after the war, however, and until then she should stay with his parents in Germany and give birth to the child there. She followed his suggestion, but instead of joining the parents of her supposed lover she ended up in an SS labor camp. From there she wrote sad letters to her parents, who subsequently turned to the priest for help in bringing about her return to Valdagno and identifying the wrongdoer in the training detachment. It then came to light that the man was guilty of other crimes, such as selling *Wehrmacht* property while posing as an Italian. On learning this, Wandel had the SS man arrested on Alga and locked up until he could be transported to *Sturmbannführer* Skorzeny.

It wasn't long before the SS man began demanding to speak to Wandel. What he had to say shocked him: the SS man did not want to be sent to Skorzeny, instead he asked to be brought before a navy court martial. After repeated inquiries as to why, the man finally broke his silence: he didn't want to be "shot while trying to escape", which meant executed by his own people as had already happened to two others, Rockstroh and another SS man who had broken into the canteen. The latter had been sent back to Skorzeny, but on the way to Oranienburg he had been shot by his SS guard "while trying to escape". Wandel doubted the story, but the SS man then provided irrefutable proof that Rockstroh had not been shot while trying to escape as claimed, but rather had been executed in his sleep by one of the guards, also a member of the SS.[105]

The facts of the case were clear to Wandel: the SS men had taken the law into their own hands without a proper court-martial, and in Wandel's eyes they were no better than murderers. On Wandel's orders, the SS men who had stood guard the night Rockstroh was killed were arrested. He sent them under guard to Admiral Heye in Timmendorf, for he no longer had any faith in the jurisdiction of the SS. Furthermore, Wandel wanted Heye to hear about the dreadful events directly from the mouths of those who had taken part. Instead of appearing before Heye in Timmendorf, however, the arrested SS men were taken straight to Skorzeny in Oranienburg. Not surprisingly, this angered Wandel even further. At the end of June Wandel and Skorzeny together reviewed the assembled combat divers on Alga, but Skorzeny had become an enemy of Wandel, who could not forgive the intrusion into his area of command.[106]

When Skorzeny immediately sent the SS men accused of Rockstroh's murder back to Alga, Wandel refused to continue their training. This was a very courageous act by Wandel, for the SS had become much more powerful and influential, especially after the attempt on Hitler's life. But it had also become clear to those in

Hauptmann Hummel leads a conversation on Alga.

command of the small battle units that this marriage to the SS must end. And yet, for the members of the small battle unit Admiral Heye "placed particular emphasis on the psychological administration of discipline. A sense of honor was consciously promoted, a sense of responsibility raised and a strong feeling of belonging created. A new type of inner discipline was visibly in the making."[107]

At the end of September the small battle unit headquarters ordered all SS and *Abwehr* members of LK 700 back to Bad Tölz.[108] This left the training detachment with the navy combat divers, with Alfred Wurzian as chief instructor, plus a few members of the *Abwehr*. A separation was also carried out in Bad Tölz: all members of the navy were removed and sent to Valdagno or Venice. Bad Tölz was now used exclusively by the SS. A second combat diver school for the SS and *Abwehr* was established in Vienna.

For Wandel himself, however, the test of strength with the SS resulting from the split between the navy and SS was not over, for his opposition to Skorzeny made him the latter's personal target. Wandel soon realized that he stood no chance in the tug of war that followed: it very soon became apparent that Skorzeny, a special favorite of Hitler's with direct access to the "Führer", was too powerful a foe. Skorzeny seized upon a recent incident and turned it against Wandel: in July 1944 Wandel had taken a business trip to the small battle unit headquarters in Timmendorf and, as the trip more or less took him to Berlin, he also paid a brief visit to his private apartment there. Skorzeny seized upon this as a breach of *Führer*

Order No. 24 – "Unauthorized Use of a Service Vehicle" – and took the matter right up to *Führer* headquarters. Himmler subsequently instructed Dönitz to initiate court martial proceedings against Wandel. Heye was able, however, to avoid a trial, which undoubtedly would have had serious consequences for Wandel, and instead had him sentenced to three weeks house arrest.[109] But Wandel's position as commander of LK 700 had become untenable. Skorzeny had achieved his goal: at the end of January 1945 Heye was forced to relieve Wandel of command of LK 700 and passed it to the detachment headquarters administration officer, Commander Hermann Lüdke.[110] A short time earlier Lüdke had led a large-scale combat diver operation in the Vistula salient. Wandel was a skilled doctor and knowledgeable naval officer with backbone, but in the end he was unable to successfully command a unit with such a variety of personnel, which constantly created conflicts of jurisdiction and petty rivalries between the navy and SS.

The conflicts between the navy and SS occurred at a time when the fronts were collapsing everywhere and "final victory" – for the Allies – was be a few months away. Wandel soon realized that not just the SS, but very soon the navy combat divers as well, would be withdrawn from Italy. On 29 September he wrote in his diary: "It is essential that we strive to transport all completed sea commando materiel to the camp in Germany in time, for if production in Italy should cease, it will hardly be possible to quickly resume production in Germany. As the combat diver arm is not strictly a combat force, but can also carry out many peacetime missions, the requirement to transport this equipment to Germany is all the more pressing."[111]

On 30 November 1944 the combat diver training detachment left its two bases in Italy, Valdagno and San Giorgio on Alba, for good. The sea commandos there were sent to Training Camp 703 in List on the island of Sylt (codename "White Belt"). Other elements of the small combat unit did, however, continue to use the installations there until just before the end of the war.

The withdrawal of Training detachment 700 from Italy also marked the end of Alfred von Wurzian's position as its head of training. Effective 26 November 1944 he was attached to the staff of the admiral in command of small battle units.[112] There he was to participate in the development of new diving equipment in the small combat force's technical department, headed by *Korvettenkapitän* Herbert Burckhardt. The experiments had two basic purposes: first, to develop a new revolutionary generation of diving equipment, and second to conduct test dives to depths of 200 meters using a helium mixture. The precise mixture of breathing gases had been very problematic, however a brand new development by Dräger promised to overcome this hurdle.[113]

Senior Engineer Hermann Tietzen of Dräger's Lübeck facility had developed an innovative automatic breathing system which it was hoped would solve the mixture problem. His innovative, highly-secret device incorporated two bellows which were activated by each breath. One chamber contained the normal mixture, which was constantly supplemented by recirculated exhaled air, while fresh, pure oxygen or helium flowed into the other. The relative size of the two bellows was controlled by an automatic spring mechanism which varied with depth, ensuring that the correct mixture flowed into the breathing bag.[114]

The question of the diving suit's insulation was discussed with Professor Peter Adolf Thiessen, director of the Kaiser-Wilhelm Institute of Physical Chemistry and Electrochemistry in Berlin. Dräger had already produced a special deep diving suit. The one-piece suit, which covered the entire body except the hands, consisted of a thick, rubber-impregnated wool web. The suit was waterproof, and was supposed to be worn with a thick insulating undergarment. The diver entered the suit through a slit in the back, which was then closed using a clamping system. In front of the face was a circular glass panel, which was screwed in place. Beneath the glass was a small suit ventilation valve. The suit incorporated a rubber breathing mask which covered the nose and mouth. The breathing hose was screwed onto the breathing mask from the outside.[115]

Dr. Herman Becker-Freysing, director of the *Luftwaffe*'s aviation medicine research department, was supposed to be brought into the experiments with the new diving equipment and the use of hyperbaric gas mixtures. Becker-Freysing had previously carried out ground-breaking research into the use of pressurized gas and oxygen saturation.[116]

Wurzian was unable, however, to carry out his new duties as a test diver for new developments to the extent planned – helium gas had by then become available in sufficient quantities, but there was a shortage of testing equipment and suitable deep diving sites. The navy thus failed to achieve a breakthrough, and like so many other German secret projects, "Sea Spirit" could not be brought to fruition before the war ended.[117]

With the transfer of Training Detachment 700 from Italy to List, further training of sea commandos became a special problem. Located off the Danish coast, List was Germany's most northern outpost, far from civilization. It possessed a very important port, which was accessible regardless of tides. The North Sea port of List was therefore of enormous strategic importance throughout the Second World War. The First World War had seen the construction of a seaplane base east of the old town center. In the 1920s this was used as a commercial flying school and at the end of the 1930s it underwent considerable expansion for the *Luftwaffe*. The port of Lister was also laid down at that time and barracks and houses built for *Wehrmacht* personnel.[118]

With the transfer to Sylt, new facilities had to be found for sea commando training and exercises. On Alga training activities had already had to be sharply reduced because of the onset of stormy winter weather, but at least the pool in Valdagno was still available. While a shortage of coal meant that the water could no longer be heated properly, it was still warm enough to conduct diving practice. On Sylt, however, training was impossible: there was no suitable swimming pool, and in December the cold, murky North Sea was out of the question for open-water training.

Practical exercises and diving equipment function tests could only be carried out on a limited basis in the Königshafen, List's protected harbor. Königshafen is a bay, about 4.2 square kilometers in size, bordered to the north by an area of dunes and to the south and west by marshland and dikes respectively. It is very flat and almost everywhere shallow enough to stand in even at high tide. The current in the tideway when water flows in or out is not to be underestimated. At low tide almost three-quarters of Königshafen's area is dry.

The development of the war in its final phase led to a change in the combat diver mission. The focus was no longer on sea operations, but rather on river missions against enemy bridgeheads. While the small battle force was initially able to concentrate on pure diving missions and leave matters of transport to and from the target to the navy, now the specialized naval unit had to be transformed into an "amphibious" force trained for tactical cooperation with the army.

The small combat force had to look about for a suitable location in which to resume its training. The large swimming pools in the SS officer school in Bad Tölz and the Diana Pool in Vienna were already being used by the SS and were thus unavailable. At the end of January 1945 Wandel performed his last task as commander of LK 700: to organize the creation of a combat diver school for river operations in Breslau. While Wandel did reach Breslau, the front was already approaching rapidly, and he barely managed to escape the city, which had been declared a fortress.[119] As Breslau had to be abandoned, the small battle force now planned to establish a replacement school for LK 700 in Dresden. But once again its plans were negated by the approach of the front. This meant that there was no systematic training of combat divers from the time the Italian training camps were abandoned until the end of the war.

By war's end Training Detachment 700 had trained about 400 combat divers. In Wurzian's estimation, only about 90 of these men, who had attended the sea training camp on Alga, were really fully trained. And of these 90 combat divers, 60 at most were actually committed to operations.

CHAPTER NINE

COMBAT OPERATIONS

As soon as strategically-important objects in enemy territory, such as ships at anchor or harbor entrances, or inland objects like locks or bridges which could not be destroyed by conventional means, were reported, Admiral Heye was given orders to commit his combat divers. The operational orders usually came from the OKW's operations staff under *General* Alfred Jodl. Not only were the lone warriors of the small battle force under him, but the military units of the *Waffen-SS* as well.

The missions themselves were carried out by marine operational commandos (MEK), each consisting of a commander and two squads of eleven men each. Their predecessor was the "Black Sea Marine Operational Commando", which had been established in June 1941 under Commander Dr. Armin Roth as part of a combined operation between the *Decima Mas* and the German navy. Prior to the founding of the small battle force, the *Abwehr* had also had a marine operational commando. When the small battle force was formed, it took over the mission from the *Abwehr*. In the course of time further operational commandos were formed. These followed the example of MAREI and MARKO, two marine commando units formed by the *Abwehr*'s Hamburg office. They retained the designation "Marine Operational Commando", however they were assigned the abbreviation MEK and a number. The only permanent members of the MEKs were their officers, while other personnel were determined by existing possibilities, requirements and availability of volunteers.[120]

On paper the military organization of the small battle units looked structured and logically organized, however in practice it was quite unorthodox, changing frequently to meet requirements. Most units were only formed just prior to an operation. Their members were recruited from the respective training detachments, the motor vehicle battalion and from mechanics and ground personnel. All personnel had to volunteer for each mission, and they were only permitted to take part if they were completely healthy.

In addition to effective weapons and equipment, the physical capabilities of the combat divers were supposed to be confirmed and, when possible, enhanced. A report by naval staff doctor Dr. Richert on the "Health Situation of the Small Battle Force and the Hygiene of the Lone Warrior" reveals "that a marine commando burns approximately 4,990 calories in 24 hours, about twice as many as a normal civilian".[121] The combat divers, who were on excellent rations to begin with, received special additional rations prior to a mission. This included food which was high-protein and low-residue, to obviate the need for bowel movements during operations. The combat diver's diet also included a high proportion of fat, like the crews of miniature submarines. In March 1944 Admiral Heye held a meeting which was attended by navy staff physician Dr. Armin Wandel in his capacity as medical officer of the marine operational commandos. Heye called for the development of a performance-enhancing drug which would allow the combat divers to cope with the effects of fatigue and exhaustion. In his words, it was to "maintain the operational fitness of those soldiers who, as lone warriors, would have to perform longer than normal, by simultaneously raising their feeling of self-worth and mobilizing their reserves of strength".[122] Also present was navy staff physician Prof. Dr. Gerhard Orzechowski, who later led the pharmacological department of the Naval Research Facility for Submarine Medicine in Carnac. He went so far as to demand a preparation that would "turn a man into a beast of prey".[123] A drug which kept the combat diver alert and awake was urgently needed, both to enable him to complete his mission and return safely.

Designated "D IX", the new drug for the small battle force was in part based on Pervitin (1 – phenyl – 2 – methylaminopropan), produced by the Temmler Company. There is little evidence that D IX was actually used, and the use of stimulants on operations by the combat divers of Training Detachment 700 cannot be confirmed.

Another performance-enhancing preparation was supposed to improve night vision. With the assistance of *SS-Hauptsturmführer* Dr. Wetz, experiments were carried out with two variants: the first, algae-based, was supposed to improve night vision by a factor of 8 to 10, while the second preparation, based on deep-sea fish, was even supposed to produce a 40-fold improvement. These experiments could not be brought to a satisfactory conclusion before the war ended, however. Nothing is known about the possible use of these preparations in action.[124]

In addition to improvements in the physical fitness and performance of the combat divers, consideration was also given to steeling them mentally. One way was to purposely bring them to, or even beyond, the brink of panic during practice dives. A second objective was to allay their fear of sharks. To this end the "Monaco Plan" was initiated at Valdagno in early May 1944. In planning future missions Alfred von Wurzian and Friedrich Hummel wrestled with the problem of determining the level of threat sharks might pose to combat divers. Wurzian had been able to gather valuable knowledge about the behavior of sharks and possible defenses against them during his expeditions with Hans Hass, however these findings were unconfirmed and the defensive measure of "approaching and shouting" did not always work. During the Aegean expeditions Wurzian had discovered that the sharks there had become so used to loud explosions produced by local dynamite fishermen that shouting did not always frighten them. He therefore feared that sharks in a combat zone would have become desensitized by the sounds of gunfire. There was thus no universal shark defense which could provide combat divers with the necessary protection during missions.[125]

The "Monaco Plan" called for providing the small battle force with a scientific research cell which would develop and test a new shark defense method and conduct scientific studies into shark behavior. This new shark defense method would subsequently be used to protect combat divers, the crews of ditched aircraft and survivors of sunken ships.

Genoa and Monaco were considered as locations, as both offered marine research facilities. Italy already possessed a similar, though rather technically-oriented research station headed by Captain Angelo Belloni. It worked closely with the Pirelli factories in Milan which produced the Italian breathing devices and other items of equipment such as fins and diving suits. The Allied advance in Italy and their invasion of southern France in August 1944 made the use of the stations in Rapallo and Monaco impossible, however, and the plan was not realized before the war ended.

The long-awaited Allied offensive had begun in spring 1944. The enemy had broken through the southern wing of the German front in Italy, forcing the abandonment of the "Gustav Line". As a result Rome fell into Allied hands without a fight on June 4th. The Allied landings in Normandy took place on June 6th while the German defenders in Italy were withdrawing to the "Green Line", which extended from La Spezia across the Apennines to Rimini in Upper Italy.

The invasion of Normandy and the rapid advance by the Allies prompted the first combat diver operations. The first mission orders reached Training Detachment 700 soon after Wandel assumed command: on 21 June 1941 Admiral Heye ordered the immediate commitment of combat divers on the invasion front.

Wandel's subsequent discussion with Hummel and Wurzian revealed that while Wurzian considered his men sufficiently well trained for an operation, Hummel felt exactly the opposite and asked that the small battle force not be made operational until 20 July 1944. Wandel subsequently sent a telex to this effect to Heye's chief of staff, but Hummel's request was ignored. *Leutnant* Opladen contacted Hummel by telephone and verbally ordered him to immediately send his best combat divers to the mission location.

Further discussion was now pointless, and after gathering the volunteer submissions, Hummel and Wurzian together decided which divers would take part in the mission. Wurzian wrote: "The divers themselves were enthused, and those who had once fought tooth and nail against being sent on a 'suicide mission' allowed themselves to become caught up in the adventure of these missions. They saw them in part as sport; a dangerous sport to be sure, but one which offered the imagination limitless scope. They felt confident and well-trained."[126] Furthermore the men were under no pressure to actually carry through the mission. "The combat divers would approach the target completely on their own. It was thus impossible for anyone to check whether they had in fact reached the target. Each man could turn around and swim back if he wished, and no one would be in a position to make accusations. Even military conditioning was of little help," recalled Wurzian.[127]

Wurzian placed his own name on the list of volunteers, determined to take part in the first action by his force. Immediately after the list was forwarded to the small battle force's headquarters, however, a telex was received: the chief of staff, Commander Fritz Frauenheim, expressly forbade Wurzian from taking part in the operation. His justification was that, as an expert and instructor, Wurzian was irreplaceable. Wurzian disobeyed the order, however, and left for the invasion front with the other combat divers under the command of Friedrich Hummel. The combat divers' baptism of fire would see them attempt to blow up the bridges over the Orne Canal and River near Benouville, six kilometers north of Caen.

Hummel, Wurzian and ten combat divers departed Venice for Caen in three Lancia touring cars. Between Dijon and Paris one of the cars collided with a truck. Four men, including Hummel, suffered minor injuries and had to be left behind in hospital. On the road from Paris to Caen the other two cars almost fell prey to enemy aircraft, but at the last second the drivers turned into a forest lane and concealed the vehicles.

On arriving in Caen they met *Oberleutnant* Hans-Friedrich Prinzhorn, leader of MEK 60, who had been designated their mission commander. Prinzhorn had been a staff officer in Navy Operational Detachment Black Sea at the same time that Heye was chief of staff of Navy Group Command South. Not only did he know Heye well, he was also an "old hand" in combat diver commando operations. Prinzhorn's job had been to coordinate operations by the *Decima Mas* and the *Kriegsmarine* detachment in the area around Sevastopol.

The combat divers divided themselves into two groups of three. The first group, consisting of *Feldwebel* Karl-Heinz Kayser, *Funkmaat* Heinz Bretschneider and *Obergefreiter* Richard Reimann, was given the job of blowing up the bridge over the Orne Canal. The second, made up of *Oberleutnant* Sowa, *Oberfähnrich* Albert Lindner and *Fähnrich* Ullrich Schulze, was assigned the bridge over the Orne River. The canal and river were about 400 meters apart at the bridge site. Prinzhorn and Wurzian stayed behind on the bank at the entry point.

Late on the evening of June 22 two heavy torpedoes, each weighing 1600 kilograms, were slipped into the water. They had been delivered by the shipyard in Kiel and had been set to run half a meter below the surface of the water. The fitters had not calculated on a river operation, however. As fresh water is less buoyant than salt water, the torpedoes immediately sank to a depth of several meters. Several empty gasoline cans were hurriedly strapped to the torpedoes to provide added buoyancy. Thus modified, the torpedoes were made relatively stable, but the cans stuck part way out of the water and made swimming extremely difficult. There was little more that could be done, as time was critical and the area was also under artillery fire.

The first group under *Feldwebel* Kayser set off down the canal towards the target. It had a long way to go: 24 kilometers altogether, 12 there and 12 back. Kayser and Bretschneider led the way. In each hand they held a tow rope, with which they towed the torpedo against the gentle current. Reimann brought up the rear, steering the torpedo. His was the most difficult task: one of the rear gasoline cans was leaking and the aft part of the torpedo gradually began to sink. Reimann finally had to stand on the bottom with his shoulder under the torpedo in order to keep it in a relatively horizontal position.

There was great relief when the bridge finally appeared. The team reached the bridge, anchored the torpedo to a piling and headed back toward German territory, the current now with them. The divers reached their departure point shortly before dawn. The torpedo exploded at the planned time, but the divers' joy was short-lived. It soon turned out that a faulty sketch of the area had caused them to destroy the wrong canal bridge!

The second group under *Oberleutnant* Sowa had set off at the same time as the canal group. Sowa soon gave up, however. Unable to endure the mental stress, he turned back.[128] Lindner and Schulze were forced to carry on without him. They made rapid progress, faster than the others as the current was with them. Suddenly both men struck their heads against a wooden plank. Icy fear gripped them. Then they realized that they had reached their objective and that the wooden plank was

Combat divers helped each other put on the tight rubber suit.

Combat divers ready their equipment for an operation. Note the laced protective suit and woolen cap with camouflage net. On their feet they wear sturdy rubber shoes over their suits; the shoes were slipped into the swim fins. Prior to a mission, as much air as possible had to be removed from the breathing bag to minimize the amount of nitrogen in the system.

part of an anti-mine barricade set up a hundred meters from the bridge. They easily dived beneath it and anchored their torpedo to the bottom. The two combat divers tried to swim back but were forced to give up after a few minutes. Against the powerful current they could not possibly regain the German lines before dawn. The two men therefore left the water and hid in the bushes several hundred meters upriver from the bridge.

They were close by when the torpedo exploded. All the next day enemy patrols searched the area but failed to discover the two divers. The pair was forced to remain in this uncomfortable position until the following night. Then they crawled from their hiding place and swam across the river. Cautiously they crossed the 400 meters to the canal and then swam back unhindered, the current now with them.

The outcome of the first combat diver mission was positive: the divers had successfully carried out their orders. It was not their fault that only one of the two strategically-important bridges had been destroyed.

Back in Venice there was a dispute after the divers returned, for in planning and executing the mission Hummel had ignored and bypassed *Marinestabsarzt* Wandel, who was in fact the new detachment commander. Wandel encountered tremendous difficulties gaining acceptance as new commander of the detachment.

Synchronizing watches before an operation.

Hummel had yielded the seat of detachment commander only reluctantly when Heye promoted Hummel over his head. As well, Hummel was highly regarded by the men of the training detachment on account of his practical experience. Many of the men could not believe that a doctor was to be placed in charge of their special unit and some openly rejected the idea.

Exhausted, the group returns to land after the operation.

Wandel was faced with a *fait accompli* when he heard that his best combat divers had left with an unknown destination and mission. This meant that training of the remaining members of his detachment would have to be curtailed. Wandel was boiling inside, and when his telex to the chief of staff with a complaint about Hummel's behavior went unanswered – as members of the *Abwehr*, Hummel and Wurzian were outside the disciplinary authority of the navy – he decided to go to Timmendorf and put his case to Admiral Heye in person. This official trip from Venice to Timmendorf would later result in the court martial against him launched by the SS.

Wandel's complaint against Hummel voiced personally to Heye also achieved nothing, and the friction between the two men continued until Hummel left the training detachment in early September to take over a newly-formed SS combat diver detachment. Only then was Wandel able to achieve his goal of full command of Training Detachment 700. Until then Hummel had led an operational detachment (the so-called "Operational Group Hellmer") within Training Detachment 700, carrying out individual missions, in the mouth of the Orne River and Le Havre, for example.

On 19 July Training Detachment 700 received orders for an operation against the Italian ports of Ancona and Livorno. Ancona was already in enemy hands and Livorno was about to fall. As planning for such an operation by combat divers required several days, there was no time for a mission against Ancona. As well, the detachment was still waiting for igniters and blasting caps to arrive from Borletti in Milan. The Borletti time-delay detonators were an Italian product and the recesses for the igniters and blasting caps were scaled for Italian components, consequently German-made items would not fit.

As the fall of Livorno and La Spezia to the Allies was expected soon, the next day Wandel sent six combat divers – four Germans and two Italians under *Fähnrich* Rolf Commichau – to Operational and Training Headquarters South in Sesto Calende. From there they were to be transported by truck to La Spezia with the necessary armaments and radio equipment. It was hoped that the required igniters and blasting caps could be found in the arsenal there. As well, the combat divers were to scout out the harbor and make initial plans for a future operation there. From La Spezia they were to continue on to Livorno and Viareggio and carry further operational planning in these still German-held ports. No fuse components were found in La Spezia, however, and as no final operations order was received from the naval command the combat divers were immediately sent back to Venice.[129]

Wandel wanted to deal similarly with the other important ports still in German hands like Genoa and Venice: an on-the-spot examination, location of landmarks suitable for orientation by day and night, and the establishment of entrance and exit

An operations team enjoys the first cigarette after a safe return. From left to right: unknown, Hans Greten, Walter Lewandowski, Dr. Wandel, unknown, Johann Gothe and Coor.

routes. Gasoline had become so scarce, however, that the drives to the ports could no longer be carried out. Preventive operational preplanning was thus impossible, except for the ports of La Spezia, Genoa and Venice. Fuel allocations were reduced even further in the second half of 1944, and sometimes the situation made it impossible to make regular pick-ups of oxygen from the plant in Vicenza.

With the shortage of fuel needed to transport the combat divers to a designated combat location and especially of reliable fuses for the explosive charges, by the autumn 1944 it was becoming difficult to justify the continued existence of Training Detachment 700. The main role originally envisaged for the combat divers, neutralizing enemy ships in harbor, was no longer possible, and it was ultimately relegated to second place behind river operations.

The shortage of time-delay detonators was surely one of the main problems facing the sea commando unit, but in the beginning it also had to grapple with inadequate supplies of diving equipment. Not until the end of July was the long awaited for diving gear received from Milan. It was of such poor quality, however, that Wandel noted in his diary on 21 July 1944: "Many of the sets delivered by the companies have problems. Workmanship is poor, the parts fit badly and valves and seals leak. The filters on the potassium capsules have been not been soldered carefully enough or not at all, causing potassium to fall into the breathing bag. The delivered compasses have inadequate illumination and cease to function if tipped even slightly. Some of the diver's watches, which are supposed to have been tested to 4 atm, begin leaking at 1 to 2 atm."[130]

On 26 July a night exercise was carried out with swimming through the canals of Venice, completing the training of the first 20 naval detachment personnel. Each man was given his own diver's watch as an outward symbol of this and they had earned the right to call themselves "combat divers". From November 1944 each fully-trained combat diver was also permitted to wear the newly-created "Certification Badge of the Small battle units". It consisted of a stitched golden sawfish and was worn on the upper right arm. It was intended to symbolize the nature of the small battle units' operations.

On 28 July eleven combat divers under the command of *Oberfähnrich* Harald Wirth were sent to the small battle unit headquarters on Timmendorfer Beach in preparation for an operation.[131] Aerial reconnaissance had discovered that the English had stored large quantities of supplies in the area of the Orne locks. Destruction of the locks would flood the area and destroy the supplies. The use of combat divers was possible as the locks could be accessed from the English Channel.

Final preparations were made in the positions of a naval artillery battalion on the Channel Coast. Extra caution would be required, as it was assumed that the enemy would have strengthened his guards after the attacks on the Orne bridges. Just before midnight eight men under *SS-Obermaat* Orlowski swam into the lock with two torpedoes. They reached the lock gates undetected and both torpedoes were anchored on the bottom in front of the gates. The time-delay detonators were armed and the sea commandos swam back to their entry point unhindered. The two torpedoes detonated on time and destroyed the lock gates on the Orne. Another mission had been successfully completed.

In the period from just before the invasion until the end of the war, MEK 60 under Prinzhorn carried out a total of 24 operations. Most were successful, but from a military point of view they failed to have the desired effect, for wrecked bridges and canal locks scarcely hindered the Allied advance. The operation by MEK 60 against the "Vasouy" coastal battery, which fell into enemy hands intact in late August 1944, is typical. Located on the south bank of the Seine estuary between Honfleur and Troutville, it threatened German-occupied Le Havre on the north bank. On the night of 26 August 1944 Prinzhorn and seven sea commandos made a daring crossing of the Seine with explosives-laden boats and blew up the guns in the battery. It was a pyrrhic victory, however, for a few days later the Germans had to abandon Le Havre and the coastal battery thus ceased to be a threat.

The war's progress had the effect of limiting the effects of many operations by the marine commandos, however this in no way diminished their accomplishments.

This sentiment was reflected in a telex sent to "Operational Group Hellmer", the operational component of Training Detachment 700 led by *Hauptmann* Hummel, by Admiral Heye on 24 August 1944:[132]

> *Radio message from Small battle unit Headquarters for Operational Group Hellmer on 24 August 1944:*
>
> *To Replacement and Training Headquarters South for Operational Group Hellmer:*
>
> *To you and your sea commandos I express my utmost appreciation. Even if we were denied military success, that is not the fault of you and your men. For me the decisive thing is the soldierly act and the willingness for action it demonstrates. Your have provided clear proof of this. We now know what we may expect of the sea commandos. – Keep it up!*
>
> *signed Heye*

At the beginning of September 1944 Wandel summed up the lessons learned from the operations carried out to date:

The eleven-man operations team commanded by Oberfähnrich Wirth returns home after its successful mission on the invasion front (Orne locks) on 29 August 1944. Seen here in Alga's harbor, the men receive an enthusiastic welcome from their comrades and are immediately called upon to tell about their experiences.

"1. The most difficult aspect of an operations is provision of means of transport. The sea commando's maximum radius of action is 5 nautical miles, which takes 5 hours to cover. Under the currently-existing coastal and harbor conditions operations are severely limited if a mode of transport is not available which can deliver the sea commandos to the immediate vicinity of the target area.

2. Operations by sea commandos cannot be improvised. Thorough preparations are required for a reasonable chance of success and to also give the men a chance of making it back.

3. To date trained sea commandos have been available for operations, however some items of equipment are still lacking:

a) a usable compass,

b) depth gauges, which previous experience has shown are indispensable,

c) sufficient quantities of explosive packets and time-delay fuses for the conduct of operations on a large scale.

4. In general, operations against port and shipping targets can only be carried out during the warm times of year in relatively calm seas if the sea commandos are required to cover longer distances in open water. Cold water trials in the Valdagno swimming pool revealed that operational endurance for sea commando operations drops rapidly at water temperatures below 17 degrees Celsius.

5. Therefore the employment of sea commandos does not need to be limited to ship targets in port or on the open seas, which often require very long periods in the water. They may be used anywhere water is present, including rivers and lakes. If cold times of year and the military situation place limits on sea operations, there are still sufficient worthwhile possibilities for sea commandos such as the destruction of bridges, dams, locks etc., and large and small assault operations, some of which can even be carried out during the cold times of year."

The course of the war made it appear likely that the greater percentage of future operations would take place in rivers and lakes, consequently cold protection for combat divers would have to be improved.[133] A reference to an improved diving suit for operations in cold water appears in the medical log of the small battle force's medical officer, Dr. Hans-Joachim Richert. The suits worn by combat divers were to be optimized in cooperation with Prof. Holzlöhner, a *Luftwaffe* medical officer, as operations in low water temperatures were imminent.[134] Therefore in September 1944 tests were begun with a *Luftwaffe* rubber suit. It was found to have excel-

Above: Training Detachment 700 assembled on the parade square on Alga for the presentation of Iron Crosses. Note the barracks still under construction.

Opposite
Top: Feldwebel Karl-Heinz Kayser and Obergefreite Richard Reimann receive the Iron Cross, Second Class. Bottom: Oberfähnrich Wirth's operations team received the first decorations awarded to members of Training Detachment 700.

lent insulation and flotation properties and its adoption was recommended. At a temperature of 2 degrees Celsius the suit prevented hypothermia for a period of at least one hour. As well, in November Training Detachment 700 received for testing three examples of a new underclothing made of wool plush which had been developed by the German Research Institute for Textile Industry under Prof. Dr.-Ing. Mecheels.

September 1944 was to be the most successful month of all for the combat divers. By then they had amassed sufficient operational experience and improved their attack methods. As well they had a new a new weapon designed especially for use in rivers: the torpedo mine. The cigar-shaped weapon was about five meters long. Its light metal hull consisted of three chambers. One housed Nipolit high-explosives and a time-delay fuse which could be preset on land and then activated at the target by pressing a button. The other two chambers, at the front and rear, were filled with ammonia gas which provided buoyancy and could easily be flooded in the target area. Its precisely balanced buoyancy allowed the mine to float just beneath the surface of the water. The buoyancy could be adjusted using a small threaded cylinder. Tow ropes were attached to the mine to allow the divers to pull it behind them. The mines were painted brown to make them resemble driftwood.

On 7 September small battle unit headquarters summoned all available combat divers for a major operation in the Low Countries. On Alga 22 men volunteered and two groups were hastily formed. For security reasons the two groups were ordered to depart by different routes. The first, consisting of eleven men under the command of *Obermaat* Orlowski, departed from Limena near Padova. The second group was also made up of eleven men and departed from Venice under the command of *Feldwebel* Karl Schmidt. The two groups' targets were located in the same region: the Nijmegen bridges and the Antwerp locks.

"Operation Market Garden", a large airborne landing operation near Nijmegen and Arnhem by British forces under Field Marshall Montgomery, had created a dangerous bridgehead across the Waal, one of the branches of the Rhine, in Holland. The retreating German forces failed to destroy the two bridges over the Waal, one a railway bridge and the other a massive road bridge. Now combat divers were to attempt to destroy these strategically-vital bridges in the enemy rear in order to delay the advance of the British forces.

The group under *Obermaat* Orlowski reached the Nijmegen operations area and there met *Oberleutnant* Prinzhorn, who was to lead the attack on the Nijmegen bridge. The detachment set up its quarters in a barn, part of an old brickworks, upstream on the east bank of the river, and began operational planning. *Hauptmann* Hummel arrived unexpectedly almost at the same time as the detachment. He produced an order signed personally by Adolf Hitler which called upon the combat divers to give their best and placed Hummel in personal command of the operation.

The men of the detachment were astonished, for Hummel had ceased to be part of Training Detachment 700 several days earlier. Now, under Otto Skorzeny, he commanded the separate combat diver group of the Reich Central Security Office. It had undoubtedly been Skorzeny himself who had approached Hitler to request that the SS be placed in charge of this important operation, thus underlining his responsibility for important operations in the interior. This was also a small measure of revenge for Skorzeny for the separation from the SS initiated by the navy.

Oberleutnant Prinzhorn was affronted by the sudden loss of his command and he telegraphed Admiral Heye requesting a new assignment. Prinzhorn was withdrawn from Nijmegen and placed in command of the second group of combat divers assigned to the lock gates of Antwerp.

The destruction of the Nijmegen bridges would be the German combat divers' most difficult mission so far, for the currents were powerful and there was little information on local conditions. The bridgehead was about 15 kilometers wide, and the Waal flowed in an arc through it. On both sides of the bridges the combat divers had to cross approximately seven kilometers of enemy territory.

In a stroke of luck the detachment came into possession of design drawings of the bridges and these were used to determine the explosive charges to be used. The road bridge in particular was unusually large with extensive supports, and an unusually large quantity of explosives would have to be used to achieve success. This further increased the difficulty of the mission.

To gain an impression of the situation and the currents at the bridges, Hummel carried out a solo scouting mission. After dark he entered the Waal near the brickworks and allowed the current to carry him 15 kilometers downstream under the two bridges and back into German territory. Hummel was not discovered, and after his return he reported that the English had extremely strong security measures in place.[135]

It had become clear to Hummel that the first bridge he had passed, the massive road bridge, could only be destroyed by an extra-powerful explosive charge. He calculated that a single torpedo mine would suffice for the railway bridge beyond it.[136] Hummel divided his detachment accordingly: four men with a torpedo mine

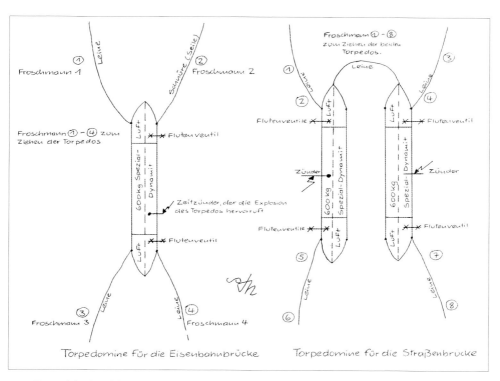

Hummel, leader of the operation against the Nijmegen bridges, later sketched the torpedo mines used and their rope connection.

for the railway bridge and eight men with two torpedo mines for the road bridge. Each of the mines was filled with 600 kg of Nipolit. Hummel had devised a special procedure for attacking the road bridge: a bend in the river caused the current there to be particularly strong, and it was almost impossible to make a precise approach to a bridge pier and attach the mines. His solution to the problem was to attach a long, sturdy line to the rear of each mine. As the divers approached the pier, they would position the mines to drift past on both sides, the mines and rope forming a U-shape. As soon as the trailing line made contact with the bridge support, the two mines would be stopped and drawn against the sides of the pier. After the detonators were armed and the flotation tanks flooded, the two torpedo mines would be in an ideal position for detonation. Apart from the heavy security at the bridges, the operation's biggest handicap was the fact that the combat divers had no experience in steering such a double payload in strong currents.

The torpedo mines were configured accordingly, and the attack took place on the night of 29 September 1944. The first team of four men – *Funkmaat* Heinz Bretschneider and *Obergefreiten* Walter Jäger, Gerhard Olle and Adolf Wolchendorf – entered the water and set off toward the railway bridge with their torpedo mine. They reached the bridge undetected, placed their torpedo mine and then drifted with the current downstream toward German territory. In the process the men lost sight of each other. Behind them, the torpedo mine detonated on time and completely destroyed the railway bridge. With dawn breaking, Bretschneider hid in an old boat lying on the bank. After spending the day in concealment, when darkness fell he was able to resume his journey. He reached the German lines, where he met Walter Jäger, who had arrived just ahead of him. The other two men did not return, having been captured.

The second group assigned to the massive road bridge had less luck. Led by *Obermaat* Orlowski, the group of eight was held up by artillery fire, and the men entered the water much later than planned. Initially the two torpedo mines were lashed together into a "tree trunk packet", to be separated just prior to the target. Two combat divers pulled on each of the four lines, steering the double load. The approach went well at first, but difficulties began when the bridge came into sight and the two torpedo mines were separated. The current was so strong that the two mines drifted apart uncontrollably and the divers were unable to bring them into the desired "clamp position" before reaching the pier. The only remaining option was to cut the catch lines and attempt to guide the torpedo mines into position individually. But one group was already too close to shore, and just short of the road bridge their torpedo mine struck a sandbank and became stuck. The group with the other torpedo mine missed the pier and as a last resort they sank the armed mine some distance from the pier beneath a span of the bridge. Incredibly they had not been spotted, and the men swam back to the first group to help pull the mine from the sandbank.

When all attempts to refloat the mine failed, the group gave up and armed the fuse in order to destroy it. Escape had now become a serious problem. On the one hand the group had entered the water much later than originally planned and on the other had lost much time in the unsuccessful effort to free the stranded mine. Consequently they could not drift down the Rhine as planned. The torpedo mine placed at the railway bridge about 500 meters downstream was about to go off, and the danger existed that the combat divers might pass the bridge at the exact moment of the explosion.

The eight men were forced to head back in the other direction, against the powerful current! Several hours later dawn broke, and as the divers were almost exhausted they looked for a hiding place on the riverbank where they could wait for nightfall. This was their undoing, for by talking too loudly they betrayed their position. The English at once opened fire. One combat diver was killed immediately and another sustained fatal wounds. The six survivors were taken prisoner. One of the mines exploded and damaged the road bridge. The English recovered the second mine from the sandbank and disarmed it.

Mission commander Friedrich Hummel received his first news of the outcome from Dutch radio, which in an early-morning bulletin reported that the railway bridge had been completely destroyed just as many tanks were crossing, and that the road bridge had been damaged.

This surprise attack had no decisive military significance, but its effect on the morale of the troops and civilians alike was all the greater. In spite of heavy losses – just 2 of the 12 combat divers returned – the personal efforts of the participants under extremely difficult conditions received high praise. On 2 October 1944 the combat divers received the following radio message from Admiral Heye:[137]

Radio message from Small Battle Unit Headquarters on 2 October 1944
*   To MEK 60, Training Detachment 700*
*   After several unsuccessful attempts, the important "Nijmegen bridge" has been destroyed. I acknowledge the determination of MEK 60 and of Hauptmann Hellmers in planning this operation. I am especially proud of you, my sea commandos of the Small Battle Force. You remain tough, committed and determined, true lone warriors, and this enabled you to achieve your great success. Sea commandos, you have given our force a proud tradition. Your heroic actions have set an example for the entire Small Battle Force.*

*   signed Heye, Admiral*

The two combat divers who returned from the operation, Heinz Bretschneider and Walter Jäger, were awarded the German Cross in Gold on 6 October 1944. Jäger was simultaneously promoted to the rank of *Unteroffizier*. Honors were literally heaped upon the operation's commander, Friedrich Hummel: on 19 October 1944 he was awarded the Knight's Cross of the Iron Cross for planning the operation and for his daring lone scouting mission, and then on 21 October he also received the German Cross in Gold with a simultaneous promotion to *Major*. Hummel thus became the most highly decorated German sea commando of the Second World War.

German propaganda made full use of the attack on the Waal bridges and it was also given much attention in the international press. The *Berlin Illustrated News* and its sister publication the *Munich Illustrated Press* both ran cover stories about the attack in their 30 November 1944 editions. In them German propaganda exulted, "Like the torpedo and demolition craft commanders, the combat divers are specialized fighters who have developed into sea commandos in accordance with the special rules and experiences of the war in the west. Focused completely on themselves and their mission, which they must carry out under the very noses of the enemy, they belong to the toughest class of fearless, cold-blooded lone warrior. Not even the threat of imminent death can prevent them from striking the enemy where he is most vulnerable and where surprise can celebrate its greatest triumphs."[138] The *New Vienna Daily News* even saw in the combat divers a new

German propaganda exploited the spectacular success of Nijmegen and for the first time reported publicly on the existence of German combat divers. This illustration is from an article in the Berlin Illustrated News on 30 November 1944, which described the attack on the road bridge using paired torpedo mines.

kind of human being: "They combine the virtues of an outstanding athlete with those of a death-defying soldier."[139]

In its 6 October 1944 edition, the *London Times* described the German attack on the English-held bridges over the Waal near Nijmegen as "one of the most daring operations of this war". In its final January edition of 1945, the *English Picture Post* even called the operation "the most astonishing act of heroism of the war". It went on to say: "The frogmen! A German innovation in military operations! They swam 18 miles to place their explosive charges under the Waal bridge but achieved only minimal success … What is surprising is a force which weakens the enemy side's morale as much as it bolsters that of the side that employs it. These days it is far more difficult to keep major surprise weapons secret during their preparatory phase than it was for Hannibal to conceal his elephants. In the case of the Nijmegen frogmen, the value of the surprise attack was enormous given the enemy's limited expenditure of men and materiel. The attack failed, but it taught us to be vigilant."

The sea commando operation carried out just prior to the Nijmegen attack, the strike against the locks in Antwerp, also received much attention in the press. Having been forced to hand command of the Nijmegen operation over to *Hauptmann* Hummel, *Oberleutnant* Prinzhorn had driven from Nijmegen to Antwerp to assume command of the operations group there. Antwerp was one of the biggest ports in Western Europe and of particular strategic value. The locks maintained a constant water level within the harbor regardless of tides. Every ship entering the harbor had to pass through the locks.

Destruction of the locks was only conceivable with the help of the combat divers, but it was an extremely dangerous undertaking as the locks were protected by extensive net barriers and strong tidal currents in the Schelde. These made it completely impossible for the combat divers to make a long swim to the locks. The only alternative was to use "Lentils" to transport the divers undetected to a point near the locks. The "Lentils" were small, fast, nearly silent-running demolition boats with a limited radius of action. Usually they carried nothing but explosives, but now they would be modified to transport combat divers.

The attack on the Antwerp locks took place on the night of 15-16 September 1944. Two demolition boats, their engines fitted with mufflers, were used. Each carried one officer as team leader, a boat driver and three combat divers and towed a torpedo mine. The two boats soon lost visual contact with each other in the darkness. The boat under *Oberleutnant* Dörpinghaus was the first to reach the outer area of the locks. The three divers, *Feldwebel* Karl Schmidt, *Mechanikermaat* Hans Greten and *Maschinenmaat* Rudi Ohrdorf entered the water. Towing their torpedo mine, the three men made their way to the lock gate. As they did so, Schmidt became caught

Heinz Bretschneider was one of the two combat divers to return from the action against the Nijmegen bridges. The operations team originally consisted of 12 men.

The action at Nijmegen was a great personal success for Friedrich Hummel. Within a matter of days he was awarded the German Cross in Gold and the Knight's Cross and was promoted to Major.

on an iron hook projecting from the wall of the lock and tore his rubber suit. Cold water immediately poured in, soaking his woolen suit. Schmidt had the presence of mind to allow oxygen to flow into his breathing equipment, providing sufficient buoyancy to keep him on the surface. The cold water was now a great handicap, however, and haste was required if Schmidt was to avoid hypothermia.

The three men had to negotiate several nets, but finally the 35-meter-wide lock gate lay before them. They quickly flooded the mine, anchored it on the 18-meter-deep bottom and began the swim back. As *Feldwebel* Schmidt was by then exhibiting symptoms of hypothermia, his two comrades towed him back to the demolition boat. The three exhausted divers were pulled on board and the boat headed back down the Schelde. On the way it encountered the second demolition boat commanded by Prinzhorn. It had been vainly trying to locate the entrance to the lock in the dense fog. Together the two boats headed back, and the torpedo mine at the lock gate exploded on time. Aerial photos taken soon afterwards showed that the lock gate had been destroyed, putting the harbor out of action for at least three months.

This time the combat divers had delivered a significant blow to the enemy. An English newspaper reported: "The great Antwerp lock destroyed! Yesterday the Germans claimed that their special corps of combat divers, specially equipped saboteurs known as frogmen, had blown up the main Antwerp lock." The British news agency Reuters reported: "German combat divers crippled the port of Antwerp by blowing up the lock through which all large ships must pass. Aerial reconnaissance confirms that the lock gates were completely destroyed and that shipping traffic will be halted for a long time. The Germans report that the operation was carried out under the command of *Oberleutnant* Prinzhorn, who previously destroyed the Moordeich bridge [over the Diep, a tributary of the Rhine near Rotterdam in Holland, author's note]."

Wurzian's second and last operation took place almost simultaneously with the attack on the Antwerp lock. Just a few days after the departure of the two operation groups for Nijmegen and Antwerp, Operations Headquarters South issued another mission order to Training Detachment 700. The target was enemy shipping in the port of Ancona. Wurzian came up with a special idea for this attack. He wrote: "One operation now followed another, but only against bridges, and for the most part these were successful. This one-sided style of operations did not please us in the long run, however, and so we sought new, interesting possibilities. When I heard one day that motor torpedo boats had carried out a futile attack on a port in the south of Italy, I wanted to demonstrate that divers could successfully carry out an attack against a port."[140]

On 14 September the two torpedo boats S-45 and S-71 sailed to Pula on the southern tip of Istria, each with one "Lentil" and six combat divers, the latter under Wurzian's command. The operation would be carried out from there on the night of 15-16 September. The demolition boats were modified for the operation, with large gasoline tanks replacing the explosive charges and remote control gear. From the outset, however, the mission was plagued by bad luck: soon after leaving Pula for Ancona, the torpedo boats were spotted by the enemy and forced to deploy their demolition boats 16 kilometers from the actual target. In the haste one of the boats became hung up on the deck. Thinking quickly, Wurzian drew his knife, cut the rope and jumped into the water to prevent the two boats from drifting apart.[141]

The three combat divers climbed in and set off for Ancona. After a short time, however, they discovered that their boat had sustained too much damage while being put into the water and there was no other choice but to head back to Venice. After sailing for eight hours the crew reached the mouth of the Po and, after a three-day walk, Venice. The second demolition boat fared little better: its fuel tank was damaged during launching and began leaking fuel. While the crew – *Feldwebel* Karl-Heinz Kayser, former boxing champion *Verwaltungsmaat* Micki Kühn and former master swimmer *Obergefreite* Herbert Klein – did manage to reach the port of Ancona, by then it had become so light that an attack was out of the question. They turned their demolition boat north but didn't get far. Off Fano they were discovered by the Allies, forced to stop and taken prisoner. Kayser, Kühn and Klein had had sufficient time to jettison all suspicious items of equipment, and the Allied personnel were more than a little surprised when they saw three German soldiers sitting in the converted demolitions boat wearing white woolen underwear.

In addition to combat diver operations against targets on the Italian Adriatic coast, in the autumn of 1944 attacks were also planned against targets on the Dalmatian and Croatian coasts. These were the responsibility of "Operations Headquarters Haun", for at the beginning of September the organization responsible for Training Detachment 700 had undergone a significant change. Replacement and Training Headquarters South had been split up: into "Operations Headquarters Hartmann", named for its first commander *Kapitän z.S.* Werner Hartmann, based in Pergine-Levico (for operations in or beginning from the western Adriatic), "Operations Headquarters Haun" in Triest-Opicina (for operations in or beginning from the eastern Adriatic) under *Korvettenkapitän* Schomburg, and Training Headquarters South, which was responsible for matters of personnel, training and procurement.[142]

Planning for the first operation from Pula against enemy ships in the Italian port of Bari began immediately, however the mission had to be abandoned because of the rapidly changing situation. The second plan entailed a combat diver attack against the strategically-important Dalmatian island of Lissa (old Italian name for Croatian "Vis"), approximately 50 kilometers from Split. *Seefähnrich* Schramm was detached from Training Detachment 700 to Operations Headquarters Haun to assist in preparations for the mission.

Then in mid-October ten more combat divers under the command of *Oberfeldwebel* Helmut Mitschke arrived in Pula for an operation against Lissa and Komiza Bays. The plan called for the torpedo boats to sail from Pula to a point near the port of Sibenik the first night. On the second night the divers would proceed in collapsible boats from there to just outside the bays of Lissa and Komiza. Explosive charges would be used to destroy targets of opportunity in the following order of priority: destroyers, freighters, torpedo boats. The divers would then return to their collapsible boats and be picked up the same or the following night. If necessary, they were to paddle their boats back across the sea in the direction of Cape Plocca.

The transport from Pula to Sibenik was initially delayed because of lack of fuel for the torpedo boats. Finally bad weather set in with strong, gusty winds which made the use of collapsible boats impossible, and the operation against Lissa had to be abandoned.

The Allied pipeline between Bari and Riccione south of Rimini was now selected as an alternate target. The Allies had laid a double gasoline pipeline beside the coast road. Each pipe was 19 cm in diameter. Cutting the fuel line would be a major feat. The sabotage mission was to take place in the Fano area, and once again the operation was to be launched from Pula. Following the attack, the divers were to make their way in collapsible boats from Fano along the coast to German-held territory.

The mission was conceived as a combined commando operation which, in addition to blowing up the pipeline, was also supposed to destroy the rail and road bridge at the mouth of the Metauro south of Fano. Unfortunately no transport could be found for the necessary explosives. As well a full moon phase had just begun which seriously reduced the chances of success, and consequently this plan also had to be abandoned. This was unfortunately typical of almost all combat diver operations in the autumn of 1944: there were plenty of worthwhile targets, and the enemy had not yet been sensitized by combat diver commando operations. What was usually lacking was suitable sea transport to and from the target area.

Following cancellation of these three long-range operations, in mid-October Combat Diver Group Mitschke was split up: five divers, all members of the *Abwehr*, were detached to Timmendorf under *Feldwebel* Diemann. The remaining five remained under Mitschke in Pula, and together with *Seefähnrich* Schramm they were assigned to MEK 71 under *Oberleutnant* Wolters. It was planned to employ the group from the Croatian island of Lussin (Lošinj) on scouting missions to other islands such as Silba, Olib and Premuda. These were to provide information for commando operations by MEK 71. One of these operations took place in mid-November 1944 against the port and roadstead of Silba. Other targets included the lighthouse on Gruizza (Hrid Grujica) and the marine cable station there.

Combat divers were not only called upon to carry out missions in Western Europe and the Mediterranean however. They also conducted river operations in the east. One of the first operations took place in the Baranov bridgehead on the Vistula. The Soviets had thrown numerous large bridges across the Vistula between Baranov and Pulavy. Materiel was pouring over these bridges to strengthen the bridgehead and prepare for an offensive.

The bridges had to be destroyed suddenly, immediately after the Soviets launched their offensive if possible. Grand Admiral Dönitz passed the request on to *Vizeadmiral* Heye, who in early November 1944 placed *Korvettenkapitän* Hermann Lüdke in command of the operation which had been dubbed "Operation Winnetou". Lüdke was administration officer in Heye's quartermaster staff. The mission documents convinced him that only a large-scale and very audacious attack could achieve success. The bridges would have to be blown in a single attempt, from south to north. With more than 30 bridges, two flotillas of demolition boats and a large number of combat divers would be needed.

The navy units turned themselves into pioneer troops. Preparations were extremely thorough. The attack was to concentrate on the Baranov and Pulavy bridgeheads. Two demolition boats, each loaded with 400 kg of explosives, were assigned to each bridge. The army was to undertake local feint attacks with heavy artillery support to divert the Soviets as the boats entered the bridgehead, while the *Luftwaffe* was assigned to make a mock attack on the bridges timed to coincide precisely with the start of the operation.

The decision to carry out the operation was finally made on 13 December, but the next day the first drifting ice appeared in the river. The navy requested that the attack order be issued immediately, but *Generaloberst* Harpe, commander of Army Group A, hesitated; the army command wanted to wait until the anticipated Soviet attack was even closer. Lüdke inspected the flotilla launch points to check the situation for himself. While things still looked quite favorable in the Baranov bridgehead, on 16 December he was forced to withdraw the flotillas from the Pulavy bridgehead.

Two risky aerial reconnaissance missions on 19 December revealed that kilometers-long ice barriers lay in front of the bridges, making a water operation impossible. Lüdke was able to cancel his operations order at the last minute and pull out his units. "General Winter" had won another battle for the Soviets.[143]

At the end of February 1945 on Sylt, Leutnant Alfred Keller formed the new "Combat Diver Group East" with 16 volunteers. Its purpose was to destroy Soviet supply bridges as part of "Operation Rübezahl".[144] Its first action was against the bridge over the Oder near Fürstenberg, which was the sole Soviet supply bridge into the Vogelsang bridgehead. The combat divers entered the water in Fürstenberg. Six of them, including Keller himself, swam downstream in the icy water of the Oder. Before reaching the bridge the divers encountered steel nets placed by the Soviets to guard the bridge piers against drifting mines. They nevertheless succeeded in blowing the bridge.

Combat Diver Group East set up its permanent quarters in the Baltic resort town of Ahlbeck and used it as base for further attacks. During March and April numerous difficult attacks were undertaken in Stettin harbor and important supply bridges were destroyed: two in Stettin, three between the island of Wollin and the Pomeranian mainland, and one more near Dievenow.

The last operation by Combat Diver Group East took place near Schwedt on the Oder against pontoon bridges at Nipperwiese and Fiddichow. These two bridges were the only ones in the 15-kilometer-wide sector over which the Soviets could supply their bridgehead, and their destruction would force them to abandon the bridgehead. The first mission was supposed to take place on the night of 24-25 April. A group of four divers would approach the pontoon bridge and place their 7.5-kg explosive charges. Altogether they had to swim 15 kilometers through enemy territory in the icy water of the Oder to regain the German lines and reach the mission's termination point. The first attempt was unsuccessful, as the operations group – which included Albert Lindner, who had blown up one of the Orne bridges – was put out of action by Soviet artillery fire at the entry point.[145] The second attempt, made the following night, was successful though. Just two days prior to the end of the war, on 5 May 1945, Alfred Keller and two other members of his Combat Diver Group East – Siegfried Köneke and Walter Lewandowski – were awarded the German Cross in Gold for their actions.

The combat divers continued to conduct operations until a few days before the end of the war. On 20 April 1945 Small Battle Force Headquarters reported that two groups of combat divers from "Battle Group Leather Stocking" had been moved from the west into the Magdeburg area in preparation for an attack against the Elbe bridges near Barby using mines and special explosives. According to an OKW report, the 12th Army, which was "in the formation process", had urgently requested reinforcement by all available Small Battle Force resources and also asked that all other suitable Small Battle Force assets be dispatched for use against the Russian bridgehead south of Magdeburg. Unfortunately there are no further details or information as to the outcome of these operations.[146]

While the last operation by the navy combat divers was nothing less than an act of desperation, it is interesting in that it was carried out just days before the end of the war and provided an example of these men's fearlessness. During the night of 3-4 May 1945, a force under the command of *Oberleutnant* Herbert Völtsch, who had earlier led an operation on the Rhine near Duisburg, blew up a pontoon bridge over the Elbe near Lauenburg, the only one in a 30-kilometer-wide sector. He and two other men carried the explosive devices to the bridge and submerged them. They were captured during the swim back, but they managed to escape while being transported to a POW camp in Lüneburg.

Many other operations, some of them seemingly fantastic, were planned but never carried out. For example, a midget submarine was to have been used to transport combat divers to a pipeline laid across the English Channel to the French coast by the British. The plan was to bore into the pipeline and spray an engine-destroying additive into the diesel fuel. It was hoped that this would cause much of the diesel-powered transport used by the Allies to break down.

At this point mention must also be made of one of the most important operations carried by the combat divers of the Reich Central Security Office. After September 1944, following the separation of the navy and *Abwehr*/SS, they carried out independent operations. The operational combat diver groups remained mixed units until the end of August and probably included members of the navy, *Abwehr* and SS.

After 1 September 1944 the combat divers of the Reich Central Security Office were concentrated in the so-called "SS Commando Detachment Danube", a unit within the "SS Operations Group Hungary", which was part of "SS Commando Unit Southeast". The latter formation, created in part from the former "Carpathian Raider Corps" of the *Abwehr*, was commanded by *Major* Alexander, a former *Brandenburger* now an *SS-Hauptsturmführer*. SS Commando Detachment Danube was commanded by *SS-Hauptsturmführer* Pfriemer, while the SS combat diver group within the commando detachment remained under the command of *Untersturmführer* Schreiber. The commando detachment's headquarters were initially with Operations Group Hungary in Hollabrunn-Stockerau and later in Gfoehl-Krems not far from Vienna. The Dianna Baths in Vienna were used as a training center. SS Commando Detachment Danube had about 70 personnel. About 30 of the men were from Special Operations Battalion "Oranienburg" and had been trained by Training Detachment 700 in Valdagno, Venice and Bad Tölz. The other 40 were former *Abwehr* men, including some from "Danube Guard", a unit of *Abwehr* Control Station II Southeast. *SS-Hauptsturmführer* Pfriemer originally came from Danube Guard.

In addition to SS Commando Detachment Danube, *Sturmbannführer* Skorzeny set up his own planning and command center for the organization of SS combat diver missions and placed *Hauptmann* Hummel in charge. The detachment of members of the *Abwehr* to the Small Battle Force ended at the end of August, and Hummel too transferred from Training Detachment 700 to the Reich Central Security Office – practically his old home, for the Reich Criminal Investigation Department was now Office V of the RSHA.[147] Under Otto Skorzeny Hummel became operations planner and administrator for the combat divers of the Reich Central Security Office. Skorzeny characterized Hummel as an "officer of extraordinary courage and coolheadedness."[148] In his new position Hummel went by the cover name "*Hauptmann* Wimmel".[149] Hummel alias Hellmers alias Wimmel did not restrict himself to administrative activities however; instead he continued to participate in his own combat diver operations.

The Reich Central Security Office's combat diver groups, made up of members of the SS and *Abwehr*, were not part of the *Waffen-SS'* military commando units, consequently they did not come under the command of the SS operations staff. Instead they were subordinate to the *Wehrmacht* High Command or Operations Staff. The orders to Skorzeny's units came from there, and often even directly from Hitler.

The SS combat divers' first area of operations was the Upper Rhine.[150] Following the successful Allied invasion, fears were expressed that the Allies might disregard Swiss neutrality and enter Germany through Swiss territory. This notion was raised when the German front had been stabilized in September 1944. At that time it ran roughly along the borders of the Reich. On receipt of orders from *Führer* Headquarters, Skorzeny was given several days to develop plans for such a contingency. His combat divers were to be assembled on the Upper Rhine to blow the Rhine bridges at Basel the minute Allied troops set foot on Swiss territory. This defensive measure was intended to give the German command time to establish a front and repel any attack from the neutral nation. Several weeks later the entire operation was called off and the SS combat divers were withdrawn. By then it had become clear that the Allies had no intentions of advancing through Switzerland as had been feared.

In autumn 1944 the Danube gained particular significance as a result of the Russian advance. Passing through half a dozen nations, the river now wandered in and out of the main line of resistance. Skorzeny planned to conduct a river guerilla war with his combat divers. Beginning in late summer 1944, all SS combat diver operations on the Danube fell under "Operation Trout". These were almost all surface missions, however: Commando Detachment Danube attacked Soviet tankers with mines and demolition boats. Disguised as private yachts, the boats were fitted with makeshift armor, armed with 20-mm cannon and machine-guns, and equipped with more powerful motors. By day the boats were hidden in a quiet tributary and not until night did they commence their successful operations. More than 30,000 tons of shipping were sunk on the Danube in a few months.

The last operation by SS Commando Detachment Danube as part of "Operation Trout" took place on New Year's Eve 1944. Its objective was to deliver ammunition and fuel to German troops, mainly *Waffen-SS*, encircled in Budapest.[151] The distance from the front to Budapest was approximately 60 kilometers over the partially ice-covered Danube. As the main shipping channel above Budapest had been mined, the group had to look for an alternate route to Budapest using tributaries of the Danube. The trip down the Danube was to be made using a modern motor launch, which would tow another boat. New Year's Eve was not selected by chance: it was hoped that the Russian troops would be celebrating and not notice the convoy passing downstream. The 13 SS combat divers were disguised as civilians. The crew also included a volunteer Hungarian Danube river captain and a Russian lieutenant of the Vlasov Army.

The motor launch initially made very good progress. It had already covered a good distance through enemy territory when it ran aground on a sandbank in a Danube tributary 17 kilometers from Budapest. Two combat divers were sent to Budapest in a small boat to make contact and bring back help. The men left behind in the launch had to wait two anxious days until a German boat finally arrived from Budapest. It picked up the crew and part of the launch's cargo. The rest of the cargo was transported over the next four nights.

The detachment had carried out its mission, but it was not enough to prevent the fall of Budapest, sometimes called the "Stalingrad of the *Waffen-SS*". Of the SS combat divers who took part in the mission into the encircled city, all but one were killed in the subsequent fighting. Of the 10,000 German soldiers in Budapest, just 170 managed to reach the German lines.

In December 1944 planning began for an operation by SS combat divers against the Suez Canal. To be carried out when seven or eight ships were in the canal, the attack was supposed to sink the first and the last ships and as many as possible in between. It would have rendered the vital waterway impassible for months and seriously disrupted the flow of Allied supplies. The enemy would have been forced to take the long route around the Cape of Good Hope to the Far East. The combat divers were to have been deposited by glider in the Sinai Desert and subsequently picked up again. Planning for the operation had reached an advanced stage, and specialists had even calculated the risk posed by sharks in these waters. But by the time the OKW was prepared to give the operation its blessing, lack of fuel and Allied air superiority in the Mediterranean area had rendered it impracticable.[152]

Several ports on England's west coast also contained tempting targets for the combat divers, locks for example. But these and many other plans came to nothing because of difficulties in safely transporting equipment and personnel for the attack. There was neither fuel nor transport aircraft available.

The final operation by the Reich Central Security Office's combat divers took place near Remagen in mid-March. On 7 March 1945 the Ludendorff Bridge over the Rhine near Remagen fell into American hands intact. Retreating German forces tried twice to blow it up, but the railway bridge remained standing. The first explosive charge failed to detonate. The second charge did explode, lifting the bridge slightly, but it fell back onto its abutments. Events then proceeded quickly. The first Americans crossed the Rhine at about 1600 hours and established the Erpeler bridgehead. Within 24 hours there were 8,000 men in the bridgehead on the east bank of the Rhine. It became a springboard for the Allied forces into the interior of Germany, and by seizing the Ludendorff Bridge the enemy had achieved a significant strategic success.

The Commander-in-Chief West, *Generalfeldmarschall* Gerd von Rundstedt, ordered the bridge destroyed quickly "at any price". In the following days bombers and even V2 rockets were used against the bridge, but without success. *Generaloberst* Alfred Jodl, chief of the *Wehrmacht* Operations Staff, issued orders for the sea commandos of the small battle unit to destroy the bridge.

Within the small battle unit the demolition of the Remagen bridge was code-named "*Rübezahl*". The first plan envisaged using a "Beaver", a one-man midget submarine, to deliver four torpedo mines to the bridge piers, each loaded with 700 kg of explosives. Two battle units would be committed: "Leather Stocking" under *Korvettenkapitän* Bartels and "Puma" under *Oberleutnant z.S.* Erich Dörpinghaus. The "Puma" detachment consisted of twelve combat divers, one radio vehicle with three radio operators, three troop transport trucks, one VW *Kübelwagen*, a motorcycle-sidecar combination and three trucks with trailers for transporting the torpedo mines. The operational column commander was *Leutnant* Schulz.

An attempt to launch a "Beaver" on the bank of the Rhine abeam Hönningen on the evening of 9 March 1945 failed, as Dörpinghaus' group was not equipped for this difficult task and the promised support from army engineers failed to materialize. Because of the rapidly expanding bridgehead, it was several days before Battle Group "Puma" could make another attempt. Meanwhile, by Jodl's order, the Reich Central Security Office's combat diver unit had also been assigned to the Ludendorff Bridge. An aircraft had been hastily organized to fly *SS-Untersturmführer* Schreiber and eleven SS combat divers in from Vienna.

Skorzeny was skeptical about the operation. He later wrote: "It was the first time I didn't accept an assignment unconditionally. The water temperature in the

The heavily-guarded bridge at Remagen, seen here from Erpel, was an impossible target for the combat divers. Their operation was a complete failure; the bridge was also the scene of the last operation by the combat divers of the Reich Central Security Office.

Rhine at that time was only about 6 to 8 degrees Celsius, and the American bridgehead already extended almost 10 kilometers upstream. I therefore declared that I considered the chances of success extremely low and that I would take my best men to the location and allow them to decide for themselves whether they wanted to undertake this risky mission."[153]

SS-Untersturmführer Schreiber, leader of Commando Detachment Danube's combat diver group, decided on the spot to undertake this almost hopeless mission with his men. The second attack on the Remagen bridge took place on the evening of 12 March. A total of 23 "Puma" and SS men took part. This time, however, the assault force came under heavy artillery fire while moving up to the planned entry site and the operation had to be abandoned.

It was now decided to carry out two operations in parallel: the navy detachment would try to blow up the Ludendorff Bridge with floating mines, while operation leader Friedrich Hummel, who had meanwhile arrived from Bad Ems, planned a combat diver mission to destroy the pontoon bridge near Linz, several kilometers from Remagen.

The navy detachment's new operation against the Ludendorff Bridge proved unnecessary, however, for on the afternoon of 17 March it collapsed on its own as a result of the earlier damage and the weight of Allied traffic. This had little effect on the American advance, as several pontoon bridges had been thrown over the Rhine inside the bridgehead. The navy simultaneously changed its floating mines plan to also target these bridges.[154]

Late in the evening on 17 March seven SS combat divers – *SS-Untersturmführer* Schreiber, *Rottenführer* Kretchmann, *Sturmmänner* Egelhoff, Holzmannhofer and Weidemann, and *Schützen* Vogelsang and Herbert Westbelt – slipped into the Rhine near Hammerstein. They took with them 28 packets of plastic explosive with delay fuses, four for each man. From there it was now 12 kilometers in the cold water to the pontoon bridge at Linz. The group came under fire from the left bank of the Rhine as they entered the water, and the SS men left behind on the shore heard the sound of several demolition packets exploding.

The Americans were now alerted and began illuminating the Rhine and the bridge with their powerful CDL lights (Canal Defense Lights). These operated on the principle that an extremely bright, rapidly flashing light sometimes blinds the human eye. Already on 1 March 1945, thirteen CDL-equipped tanks of the American 738th Tank Battalion had been ordered to the Remagen Bridge, which had just been captured, to illuminate the other bank of the Rhine as the bridgehead was being expanded. They were to prove a very effective counter-weapon against combat divers.[155]

Two combat divers were unable to escape the powerful lights and were forced to surrender about 900 meters north of Hönningen. They were taken prisoner by soldiers of the American 164th Engineer Battalion. When captured the two divers were carrying just their short knives, having sunk the explosives packets in the Rhine. Further downstream the Americans also pulled *SS-Untersturmführer* Schreiber and another diver from the water. The latter had been injured when small arms fire detonated one of his three-kg explosives packets. Another diver had been killed in the explosion. The exploding charge also damaged Schreiber's suit and his under-suit had become soaked in cold water. Suffering from the effects of the cold water, he and the injured man barely made it to shore.

The four prisoners were immediately interrogated. Major General Walter E. Lauer, commander of the 99th Infantry Division, which had been involved in the fighting in the Remagen bridgehead since 10 March 1945, later described Schreiber in his war report as a "fanatical Austrian Nazi, …who could only be tricked into talking after six hours."[156] During the interrogation he learned from Schreiber that two combat divers had avoided discovery.

The last two of the Reich Central Security Office's combat divers still in action were unable to place their explosives because of the illumination at the pontoon bridge, however they were able to dive beneath the nets and the bridges undetected. A reception party was waiting for them on the right bank of the Rhine near Römlinghoven (now part of Bonn). One of the divers hid out for two days in a house near Ernich, but on 20 March he was discovered and taken prisoner. Only the seventh diver managed to avoid capture.

The commando mission against the pontoon bridge at Linz was Commando Detachment Danube's finale – except for one man it had been completely wiped out. In 1992 the two surviving towers of the Remagen bridge were named historical sites and a peace museum was set up in one of the towers. The leitmotif in the peace hall reads: "Let us work every day for peace with spirit and understanding. Let each begin with himself."

CHAPTER TEN

COLLAPSE AND
NEW BEGINNINGS

The end of the war found *Leutnant* Alfred von Wurzian in List on the island of Sylt together with many comrades of Training Detachment 700. In addition to the Iron Cross, Second Class, he had been decorated with the War Merit Cross 1st Class with Swords for "outstanding service in the military conduct of the war." After his capture by a British unit, Wurzian was interrogated and soon received two surprising offers: first an American officer offered him a five-year contract if he would move to the USA and participate in a secret military program for the U.S. Army. Wurzian was not told what it was about at first, but he later learned that they wanted to use his knowledge about a new underwater breathing system under development by Dräger. Dr. Christian J. Lambertsen had been working on a similar system for the OSS, the American intelligence service, but his was not as advanced as Dräger's.

Wurzian was not the only expert to receive such an offer. "Operation Paperclip" was a secret American project begun in mid-1945. German scientists and specialists were offered entry into the USA if they showed themselves willing to work on secret projects. Many German scientists went abroad in 1945, most willingly, to conduct research for yesterday's enemy. For the technical intelligentsia of the Third Reich, especially those involved in armaments, the future was bleak in 1945. The Potsdam Agreement between the victorious powers forbade any research for military purposes in occupied Germany. Thus the elite of Germany's military researchers could only continue their work on behalf of foreign powers. More than 750 such experts went to the USA as part of "Operation Paperclip" – including Wernher von Braun, rocket pioneer and later the hero of manned space flight.

The second offer Wurzian received was from the German Mine-Clearing Service (DMRL). According to the terms of the ceasefire agreement, the Germans were responsible for clearing the mines from the Baltic and the North Sea using their own personnel and *Kriegsmarine* minesweepers. Like the first, Wurzian also turned down this offer.

Alfred von Wurzian was released by the British in September 1945 and took a position with Alnwick Harmstorf, a large diving and salvage company in Blankensee. The company was planning to establish its own oxygen diving operation. After the war every diving and salvage operation in Hamburg was hired on an hourly basis by the British military to clear the port and the Elbe. Soon afterwards Wurzian was recognized as a qualified diving instructor by the Hamburg School Authority and the professional association and also headed the city of Hamburg's oxygen diving office.

Wurzian's oxygen group started with four divers and showed promise for more than a year. Its principal task was the removal of sunken ships. Disputes soon arose, however, with the established helmet divers in Hamburg, who were losing contracts to Wurzian with his simple, free-diving work methods. In February 1947 the shed in which he kept his equipment was broken into and most of it stolen. He thus lost his entire basis as an independent career diver.

The underwater career which had begun as a member of Hans Hass' expedition in 1939 was now over, and Wurzian began building on his original profession. In summer 1947 he went to work for a company producing powdered baby formula. As project director, he oversaw the construction of two new factories. At the same time, he began working on a five-year expansion plan for the of the port of Hamburg on behalf of the Hamburg Senate. He later became a leading salesman for a beverage company in Winsen and the Stülcken shipyard in Hamburg.

In the mid-1950s Wurzian moved to the Krupp Company in Essen. Together with his wife and two children, he moved to India, where the company was constructing a large iron and steel mill in Rourkela. After five years abroad, he stayed with the company's head office in Essen for several years before moving back to Vienna, his home town. In 1965 he became the general manager for Austria in Operation VARTA. A few months after taking this new position, Wurzian suffered a stroke, a delayed effect of his intensive oxygen diving during the war. His speech was affected and he was forced to leave his position. He gradually regained his speech before his death in 1985, but he had paid a high price for realizing his dream of a German combat diver force.

After 1945 the lesson learned in the Second World War, that determined, well-trained combat divers could achieve decisive results, led to the formation of similar elite formations in most militaries. In 1950, during the Korean War, the

USA expanded its combat diver force even further and soon founded the SEALs (SEAL = sea, air, land), excellently-equipped and trained combat divers who first saw service in the Vietnam War. For their part, the French used the famous "*Nageur de Combat*" units in the Indochina War, and the British formed a maritime component of the SAS, the SBS (Special Boat Service).

Following the concepts of modern armed forces, in 1959 the *Bundeswehr* established a new combat diver group. It made sense to build on the experience of the former *Kriegsmarine* combat divers as well as those of allied nations, especially France. On 1 July 1959 in List on Sylt, *Kapitänleutnant* Günter Heyden, *Kapitänleutnant* Herbert Völsch and *Oberbootsmann* Walter Prasse, all former Second World War sea commandos, began the first course with a strength of three NCOs and ten officer candidates. Heyden became the first commander of the new combat diver unit. Until his retirement in September 1967, Völsch was responsible for the training of all *Bundesmarine* combat divers. After several base changes, the combat diver platoon was moved to its present-day base in Eckernförde and in 1964 it became an independent company.

The equipment used by modern combat divers has undergone enormous improvement, but defensive measures have also become much more lethal. Naval

Veterans of Training Detachment 700 gathered in Eckernförde to mark the tenth anniversary of the formation of the Bundesmarine's combat diver company in 1974. In the center are Dr. Armin Wandel and Alfred von Wurzian, right in uniform Rüdiger Matzat, then commander of the navy's combat diver company.

Former top agent Friedrich Hummel at a meeting of the Knight's Cross Holders' Association in Goslar in 1986: he was the most highly decorated German combat divers and one of the outstanding characters in the history of Training Detachment 700.

units of various major powers have trained undersea creatures like dolphins, sea lions and pilot whales for military purposes, such as espionage, the location of lost torpedoes, defense against or killing of enemy divers, and carrying of messages.

Accounts of combat divers during the Second World War and the fascinating descriptions by undersea pioneers have resulted postwar in an unprecedented human invasion of the oceans. In Germany, Austria, Switzerland and England, it was the books and films by Hans Hass that spread awareness of the beauty of the underwater world, while in France and the USA it was Jacques-Yves Cousteau.

New branches of industry employing divers were created worldwide. In Germany in 1949, former combat divers Hans-Joachim Bergann and Kurt Ristau founded the "Barracuda Association for Water Sport" in Hamburg. Soon afterwards the first diving accessories became commercially available in Germany. What Hans Hass had first developed as a helpful method for biological marine research and was then used by Alfred von Wurzian for military purposes, developed into a new recreational activity which could be enjoyed by everyone.

ORGANIZATION OF THE GERMAN COMBAT DIVERS

Meeresjäger-Abteilung "Brandenburg"
Kommandant
Dezember 1943-März 1944   *Hauptmann* Fritz Neitzert
April 1944-Juni 1944   *Hauptmann* Friedrich Hummel

Ausbildungsleiter
Dezember 1943-Juni 1944   *Feldwebel* Alfred von Wurzian

Kriegsmarine-Lehrkommando 700
Kommandant
Juni 1944-Januar 1945   *Marinestabsarzt* Dr. med. Armin Wandel
Februar 1945-Ende   *Korvettenkapitän* Hermann Lüdke

Ausbildungsleiter
Juni 1944-November 1944   *Leutnant* (MA) Alfred von Wurzian

Lehrgangslager 701: St. Giorgio in Alga/Venedig
Juni 1944-August 1944   Lagerkom. *Oberleutnant* (MA) Strenge
September 1944-November 1944   Lagerkom. *Leutnant* (MA) Gerhart Kummer

Lehrgangslager 702: Bad Tölz
Juli 1944-September 1944   *Lehrgangsleiter Oberleutnant* z.S. Küsgen

Lehrgangslager 703: List/Sylt
Dezember 1944-Ende   unknown

Lehrgangslager 704: Valdagno
Juni 1944-November 1944   Lagerkom. *Oberleutnant* (MA) Herbert Völsch

Einsatzleitung Kampfschwimmer RSHA Abt. VI-S
September 1944-Ende   *Hauptmann* Friedrich Hummel[157]

SS-Jagdkommando Donau
September 1944-März 1945   *Untersturmführer* Walter Schreiber

NOTES

1. Reader's letter in the WamS of 16 FY 1956.

2. Ochwadt, Curd: *Das Steinhuder Meer*, Hanover, 1967.

3. Alfred von Wurzian (24/09/1916 - 21/01/1985). One of his ancestors was Joseph Ritter von Wurzian (1805-1858), personal physician to the famous Field Marshall Graf Radetzky (1766-1858).

4. Interestingly, according to a patent by the Italian Mario Moschini, consideration was given as early as 1933 to using a helium-oxygen mixture (Heliox) for submarine escape devices. Patents DE 680.053 and UK 542.955.

5. Somewhat later, Heye became the commanding admiral of naval forces in the Black Sea.

6. From Schneider, Hans-Ulrich: *Das OKW muss schweigen, Teil 1*, 08/10/1951.

7. Wurzian, Alfred von: *Die Teufelsschwimmer*. 2 Parts; in Hamburger Abendblatt, supplement, 1953, BL 25/40.

8. Wurzian, Alfred von: Autobiographical writings on the period October 1942 to April 1943. Written in the years 1968-1970. Archiv Jung

9. Wurzian had seen Japanese pearl divers wearing this kind of clothing during his return from the Caribbean expedition. The divers often spent hours in the cool waters of the Pacific.

10. Wurzian, Alfred von: Autobiographical writings, ibid.

11. Wurzian, Alfred von: Autobiographical writings, ibid.

12. See Schellenberg, Walter: *Memoiren*, Cologne 1956. Armed with this knowledge, in 1942 the RSHA Abt. VI a-c sent three of its sabotage specialists to La Spezia to train with the Italian Gamma divers. They later took part in attacks by the *Decima Mas*. See Grabatsch, Martin: *Torpedoreiter, Sturmschwimmer und Sprengbootfahrer*, pp. 240 and 249. Wels 1979.

13. Leverkuehn, Paul: *Der geheime Nachrichtendienst*, Frankfurt a. Main, 1957.

14. The same principle was later employed by the "Lentil" remotely-controlled demolition boat, also developed by the *Abwehr*. It had its roots in the inventions of *Major* Goldbach, who had experimented with remote-control devices during the First World War.

15. Wurzian, Alfred von: Autobiographical writings, ibid.

16. Wurzian, Alfred von: Autobiographical writings, ibid.

17. Wurzian, Alfred von: Autobiographical writings, ibid.

18. According to personnel files, effective 01/01/1944 Wurzian was no longer with "3./Lehr-Regiment Kürfurst", but instead with "Stab Lehr-Regiment Kürfurst".

19. See Witzel, Dietrich F.: *Kommandoverbände der Abwehr II im Zweiten Weltkrieg*. In Militärgeschichtliches Forschungsamt (Publisher): Military Supplement on European Military Affairs. Edition 5, October 1990.

20. Jung, Michael: *Handbuch der Tauchgeschichte*, Stuttgart 1999.

21. Within Department II of the "Technology" Group, Mines Section. Correspondence in the author's possession.

22. In his book *Teufel der Tiefe*, Borghese (06/06/1906 - 26/08/1974) places this visit on April 1942. This cannot be correct, however, for in all likelihood this visit took place a year later, in April 1943. This conclusion fits with Eugen Wolk's accounts in Vigano, Marino: *Guerra segretta sotta I Mare. Eugenio Wolk e I "Gamma" della Decima Mas (1942-45). In Storia del XX Secolo, Casteggio (PV), No. 6-8, ottobre – dicembre 1995.*

23. Borghese, Junio Valerio: *Teufel der Tiefe*, Boppard 1961, p. 206.

24. Borghese, Junio Valerio: Teufel der Tiefe, Boppard 1961, ibid. p. 207.

25. As to the coded designation "*Abwehrtrupp 204*": the "2" stood for membership in the Auslands/Abwehr Office II, the "04" for the location Rome. After the 1944 reorganization these units were designated "frontline intelligence centers".

26. In mid-September he was awarded the German Cross in Gold for warning of the coming ceasefire and timely planning of countermeasures. Until the end of 1944 Erwein Graf Thun-Hohenstein (04/04/1896 - 12/02/1946) was head of the *Abwehr* war organization in Rome. He was recalled when the city had to be abandoned. He and his brother remained in the Italian intelligence center in Milan until the end of 1944. Toward the end of the war he commanded the *Abwehr* "Alexander" Legionary Battalion, made up of volunteers from Eastern Europe (White Russians, Ukrainians and Caucasians). He was captured by the Soviet and executed following a show trial.

27. Wurzian, Alfred von: *Die Teufelsschwimmer*, ibid.

28. After the patent "Head-free Diving Suit" by Angelo Bellini of 27/07/1934. Germany DE 665253.

29. The following information was provided by Konrad Knirim, whose standard work *Militäruhren* is highly recommended by this author for further information on this topic.

30. Schulze-Kossen, Richard: *Militärischer Führernachwuchs der Waffen-SS. Die Junkersschulen.* Osnabrück 1982, p. 71.

31. After the war Eugen Wolk and Junio Valerio Borghese were both convicted as collaborators. Wolk was pardoned however, as he made a full confession and provided considerable assistance to the Allies after the war, helping disarm mines in Venice harbor. In 1947 Wolk emigrated to Argentina and in Buenos Aires formed the military regime's combat diver unit. There, too, his work was highly successful. Wolk did not return to Europe until 1961, settling in Magliaso, Ticino on the Swiss side of Lake Lugano. He died there in the early 1990s.

32. This basic idea was realized in late 1944, but not with a submarine, instead with the armed fishing trawlers KFK 203 and KFK 204 as part of "Operation Reiserntte". See Danner, Herwig: *Kriegsfischkutter: KFK*, Hamburg 2001, pp. 53-59. The Italian divers of the *Decima Mas* had a similar idea, using the fishing boat *Cefalo*. See Borghese, Junio Valerio: Teufel der Tiefe, Boppard 1961, ibid. p. 199.

33 . Japanese combat divers constructed similar underwater strongpoints off the entrances to Tokyo in 1945.

34. Wurzian, Alfred von: Autobiographical writings, ibid.

35. Wurzian, Alfred von: Die Teufelsschwimmer, ibid.

36. Also under the command of Naval Group Command North was Naval High Command North Sea, whose commander-in-chief as of March 1943 was Admiral Erich Förste

37. Dönitz, Karl: *Zehn Jahre und zwanzig Tage*, Bonn 1958.

38. In September 1944 *Generalfeldmarschall* Albert Kesselring, Commander-in-Chief Southwest and head of Army Group C, established his headquarters in Recoaro Terme.

39. The post headquarters military postal number was L 10881 Lg. P.A. München 2.

40. According to the diary entry on 23/08/1944, made by Armin Wandel, the Gamma divers were subordinate to *SS-Sturmbannführer* Otto Skorzeny in all operational matters.

41. After the war Fritz Neitzert (21/12/1891 - 08/10/1966), codename in Valdagno "Dr. Neitzker", was manager of a knitting outfit in Bielefeld.

42. Not to be confused with the central proving battalion of the general *Waffen-SS*, the *SS-Sturmbataillon 500*. See Petersson, Ingo: *Ein sonderlicher Haufen*, Neckargemünd 1959.

43. It is noteworthy, however, that these convicted men were given back their previous SS rank if they later "redeemed" themselves at the front. This means that after carrying out a dangerous mission as an "ordinary seaman", a high-ranking officer immediately returned to his previous rank as if nothing had

happened. This proving mission was then stricken from his personnel files, making it appear that he had only been away on a "special mission" for several months. These proving missions were so dangerous, however, that many of the convicted lost their lives and never returned to the regular SS.

44. Otto Skorzeny (12/06/1908 in Vienna - 06/07/75 in Madrid).

45. As we now know with certainty, it the German paratroopers under *Major* Harald Mors who were mainly responsible for freeing Mussolini from prison on the Gran Sasso.

46. The Reich Central Security Office was the central office under SS control from which all official and secret police and security organs of the German Reich were controlled. The SS leadership in the RSHA had almost unlimited power. See Wildt, Michael: *Generation des Unbedingten. Das Führungskorps des Reichssicherheitshauptamtes*. Hamburg 2002.

47. "SS Commando Unit Center" was created from the SS Commando Battalion 502 in October 1944. The other SS commando units were formed by regionally combining the *Abwehr*'s former "Patrol Corps" units. The "Patrol Corps" were the units of the *Brandenburg* Division trained in special combat operations. Together with the SS Commando Battalion 502 and the Special Operations Battalion for Special Purposes, former *Brandenburgers* formed the bulk of the SS commando units. The SS commando units were therefore the successors to the *Brandenburger* commandos and continued their traditions.

48. It has been claimed that some SS members later took advantage of their first operation to surrender to the enemy. See Waldron, Tom J., and Gleason, James: *The Frogmen. The Story of the Wartime Underwater Operators*, London 1950, p. 148.

49. Klein, Herbert: *Es fehlt noch die Goldmedaille*. In: *Der Spiegel*, Hamburg, No. 26 of 25/06/1952. Front and back covers and pp. 23-26.

50. Wurzian, Alfred von: Die Teufelsschwimmer, ibid.

51. Wurzian, Alfred von: Die Teufelsschwimmer, ibid.

52. See Nöldeke, Hartmut and Hartmann, Volker: *Der Sanitätsdienst in der deutschen U-Boot-Waffe und bei den Kleinkampfverbänden. Geschichte der deutschen U-Boot-Medizin*. Hamburg 1996, p. 201.

53. Klein, Herbert: *Ich war ein deutscher Kampfschwimmer*. In Münchner Illustrierte, Munich, 02/06/1956 pp. 8-9.

54. Wurzian, Alfred von: Die Teufelsschwimmer, ibid.

55. The local newspaper *Il popolo vicentino* reported on it on 5 March 1944.

56. Membership in the small battle unit was kept secret and mentioned in personnel files without further comment. All that is recorded there is the date of transfer to the unit.

57. In March 1933 Friedrich Hummel (08/02/1910 - 10/07/1993) joined the NSDAP and the SA and in October 1934 was transferred to the SS. For additional information on his career also see Banach, Jens: Heydrichs Elite: *Das Führungskorps der Sicherheitspolizei und des SD 1936-1945*. Paderborn 1998; and Wagner, Patrick: *Hitlers Kriminalisten. Die deutsche Kriminalpolizei und der Nationalsozialismus*, Munich 2002. A separate biography of Friedrich Hummel is in preparation. (Jung, Michael: *Friedrich Hummel. Topagent, Kampfschwimmer, Pionier*.)

58. During his time in the military Hummel continued to be directed by the Kripo headquarters in Hamburg and Berlin and – as part of the melding of the security police (Sipo) and the security service (SD) favored by SS chief Heinrich Himmler – in the years that followed he received promotion to the equivalent of *SS-Hauptsturmführer* (30/01/1942, rank equivalent *Kriminalhauptkommissar*). At the end of January 1944 Hummel was promoted to *Kriminalrat*, a rank equivalent to *SS-Sturmbannführer*. Because of the required three-year waiting period at the previous SS rank, the promotion was not finalized before the end of the war, however. After the war and several years as an independent salesman, in 1957 Hummel joined the police force of the state of Schleswig-Holstein, becoming head of the district police headquarters in Itzehoe and, in 1964, Flensburg. In 1970 he retired with the rank of *Oberregierungskriminalrat* as head of Police Headquarters North in Flensburg. Also see Linck, Stephan: *Der Ordnung verpflichtet: Deutsche Polizei 1933-1945. Der Fall Flensburg*, Paderborn 2000.

59. See Höhne, Heinz: *Canaris. Patriot im Zwielicht*, Munich 1979, pp. 517-519.

60. Also see Schellenberg, Walter: *Memoiren*, Cologne 1956, p. 266

61. Skorzeny, Otto: *Meine Kommandounternehmen*, Wiesbaden, 1976, pp. 177-178.

62. In comparison: the *Titanic* was 46,329 gross registered tons (GRT).

63. Wurzian, Alfred von: Autobiographical writings, ibid.

64. Hellmuth Heye, born 09/08/1895 in Beckingen, Saar, died 10/11/1970 in Mittelheim, Rheingau.

65. Dönitz, Karl: *Zehn Jahre und zwanzig Tage*, Bonn 1958.

66. Bekker, Cajus [that is Hans Dieter Berenbrok]: *Einzelkämpfer auf See. Die deutschen Torpedoreiter, Froschmänner und Sprengbootpiloten im Zweiten Weltkrieg*. Herford, 1978, p. 16.

67. Skorzeny, Otto: *Geheimkommando Skorzeny*, Hamburg 1950, p. 175.

68. OKW order No. 003872/44 secret command matter WfSt/Op/Org of 15/04/1944. (BA/MA – RM 7/99).

69. The operational mission of the coastal commandos read: anti-partisan operations from the sea and commando operations across the sea behind enemy lines and against ships and port installations. See Kugler, Randolf: *Die Küstenjäger-Abteilung-Brandenburg*. In Schiff und Zeit, No. 3, 1978, p. 49 and following.

70. Skorzeny, Otto: *Wir kämpften – wir verloren*. Siegburg-Niederpleis 1962, p. 11.

71. Skorzeny, Otto: Meine Kommandounternehmen, Wiesbaden, ibid. p. 161.

72. OKW order No. 003872/44 secret command matter WfSt/Op/Org of 15/04/1944. (BA/MA – RM 7/99).

73. The school was given the military postal number M 10907 and the codename Rothenburgsort.

74. See Dal Lago, Maurizio: *L'occupazione tedesca dell'alta valle dell'Agno*, in Heinrich von Vietinghoff-Scheel, *La fine della Guerra in Italia. Appunti dell'ultimo comandante in capo Tedesco in Italia (Recoaro, ottobre 1944 – aprile 1945)*. Valdagno 1997.

75. See Dal Lago, Maurizio, and Rasia, Franco: *Valdagno marzo-giugno 1944 – Dallo sciopero generale all'eccidio di Borga*. Valdagno 2004.

76. Another combat diver school originally planned for Bled on the Blejsko, Slovakia was not realized.

77. By that time Dr.med. Armin Wandel (11/06/1913 – 25/01/1994) had already lost three brothers in the war. Two – Joachim-Friedrich Wandel (*Hauptmann* and squadron commander in a fighter wing) and Friedrich-Wilhelm Wandel (*Major* and commander of a grenadier battalion) – were wearers of the Knight's Cross. The third was Heinz-Günther Wandel (*Hauptmann* and commander of an anti-tank company). See Wandel, Armin: *Stirb und Werde*. Lahr, Schwarzwald, self-published, 1990.

78. Wandel did great postwar service in preserving and advancing knowledge in the field of submarine medicine, beginning in 1959 as *Bundesmarine* fleet medical officer and from 1962 as head of the navy's Submarine and Diver Physiological Institute in Kronshagen near Kiel.

79. Wandel, Armin: Medical Log of the Medical Officer attached to Replacement and Training Headquarters South from 03/05/1944 to 18/05/1944. Wandel estate (Archiv Nöldeke).

80. Wandel, Armin: Letter to the Admiralstabsarzt (Rtd.) Dr.med. Emil Greul dated 29/10/1990. Wandel estate (Archiv Nöldeke).

81. Wandel ordered materials for 50 sets of diving equipment. The Rosti Company delivered the woolen underwear for the Belloni suits. Most of the equipment came from Pirelli: the "Spolverini" camouflaged protective suit, the "Bovetterini" model carrying harness, sports Model 44 and Type 50 small diving outfits, swim fins, nose clamps, "Zainetta" waterproof rucksacks, watertight glasses and inflatable boats.

82. Skorzeny, Otto: Wir kämpften – wir verloren. Siegburg-Niederpleis 1962, ibid.

83. Skorzeny, Otto: Wir kämpften – wir verloren. Siegburg-Niederpleis 1962, ibid.

84. Walter Schreiber, born on 15/07/1924 in Grossraming, Steyr-Land. Postwar biography unknown; Schreiber is believed to have emigrated to Paraguay following his release from POW camp.

85. Walter Schreiber's final evaluation from the SS-Panzer-Junker Special Course of 10/01/1944 – 05/04/1944 in Fallingbostel. Archiv Jung.

86. Wurzian, Alfred von: *Die Teufelsschwimmer*, ibid.

87. Wurzian, Alfred von: *Die Teufelsschwimmer*, ibid.

88. Wurzian, Alfred von: *Die Teufelsschwimmer*, ibid.

89. Wurzian, Alfred von: *Die Teufelsschwimmer*, ibid.

90. Wurzian, Alfred von: *Die Teufelsschwimmer*, ibid.

91. Wurzian, Alfred von: *Die Teufelsschwimmer*, ibid.

92. Neumeyer had meanwhile become head of the newly-created group Amt Mil-D/T in the RSHA. His counterpart in the RSHA was *SS-Hauptsturmführer* Gerhardt, I-b in Skorzeny's operations staff in RSHAAMT VI-S. Gerhardt was responsible for all transport matters in Amt VI-S. He supplied Mil-D with Nipolit and later the "Werewolf" units with weapons.

93. Report to the admiral commanding small battle units dated 27 August 1944, Page 6. Wandel estate (Archiv Nöldeke).

94. Report to the admiral commanding small battle units dated 27 August 1944, Page 7. Wandel estate (Archiv Nöldeke).

95. Wandel, Armin: Appendix to the war diary of the commander of Training Detachment 700 from 21/06/1944 to 30/09/1944. Report to the admiral commanding small battle units dated 27 August 1944, Page 6. Wandel estate (Archiv Nöldeke).

96. Wandel, Armin: Appendix to the war diary, ibid.

97. Though assigned to the *Kriegsmarine*, Wurzian remained in the Regiment *Kurfürst* until the end of the war and was thus a regular member of the armed services. His status was also unaffected when *Abwehr II* became Amt Mil-D of the Reich Central Security Office, as the members of *Abwehr II* retained their armed services status. After the fusion with the Reich Central Security Office the Regiment *Kürfurst* came under Amt Mil, which was attached to Amt VI in the RSHA. Its commander was *SS-Brigadeführer* Walter Schellenberg. Wurzian's position title was "SS-RSHA Amt Mil Reg. Kurfürst".

98. Wandel, Armin: Detachment commander's war diary, ibid.

99. Wandel, Armin: Appendix to the detachment commander's war diary, ibid.

100. Klein, Herbert: *Ich war ein deutscher Kampfschwimmer*. In: *Münchner Illustrierte*, Munich, 02/06/1956, p. 8.

101. Wandel, Armin: Detachment commander's war diary, ibid.

102. The following descriptions are based on accounts by Dr. Armin Wandel in a lengthy letter to retired *Admiralstabsarzt* Dr. Emil Greul dated 29/10/1990. In it Wandel quotes several pages from an autobiography he was then working on. Unfortunately he was unable to publish his autobiography and according to Dr. Hartmut Nöldeke the manuscript was not passed down.

103. Wandel, Armin: Appendix to the detachment commander's war diary, ibid.

104 . Wandel, Armin: Appendix to the detachment commander's war diary, ibid.

105. The events surrounding the death of SS member Rockstroh came before the courts after the war. The case had to be thrown out, however, as none of those directly involved was still alive. As well it was impossible to find Rockstroh's grave; he had been buried without military honors outside Valdagno.

106. It is unlikely that Skorzeny thought much of Wandel from the beginning. In his autobiography Skorzeny mockingly describes an incident that took place during an evening visit by the two men to the harbor commander of Venice. Wandel, who himself steered the boat from Alga to Venice, failed to see a gondola and rammed it, whereupon Skorzeny rebuked him, suggesting that he stick to the profession for which he had been trained. See: Skorzeny, Otto: *Geheimkommando Skorzeny*, Hamburg 1950, p. 196.

107. Heye, Hellmuth: *Marine-Kleinkampfmittel*. In: *Wehrkunde*, Munich 1959, pp. 413-421.

108. According to K.d.K. order G 3600 of 21/09/1944.

109. Decree of the court, Admiral of the Small Battle Units, file Z. J 1 155/44 of 26/11/1944.

110. After the war he became an admiral in the Federal German Navy and in 1968 died in a mysterious hunting accident. It was said that he was about to be arrested on charges of spying for the Russians. Also see: Cookridge, E.-H.: *Gehlen, Spy of the Century*.1972, pp. 351-352 and 382; and Whiting, C.: *Gehlen: Germany's Master Spy*. 1972, pp. 263-267.

111. Wandel, Armin: Appendix to the detachment commander's war diary, ibid.

112. On 26/11/1944 Alfred von Wurzian received a special yellow pass, prepared for the Admiral of the Small Battle Units by *Korvettenkapitän* and chief of staff Fritz Frauenheim, which read: "Lt. (MA) v. Wurzian is a member of the *Admiral der K.d.K.*'s staff and as such has been authorized, in carrying out vital military tasks, to call upon the assistance of shipyards industries and universities as well as Reich authorities and *Wehrmacht* offices. All installations of a military and civilian nature are requested to lend him every possible assistance in the execution of his duties. The bearer of this pass is authorized to wear civilian clothes, use express trains carrying frontline soldiers home on leave as well as all express trains, and carry a firearm."

113. The Royal Navy also experimented with artificial breathing gas mixtures. They used an oxygen-nitrogen mixture (Nitrox with 32% to 60% oxygen). This reduced the danger of oxygen poisoning while increasing the maximum diving depth to about 30 meters. Nitrox is not a deep-diving gas, however. A helium-based mixture of gases is the solid favorite for this purpose.

114. This was the direct predecessor of the Dräger firm's automatically-controlled breathing device dubbed the "LAR III". After the war it would become standard equipment in all western military diving units. LAR equipment is still the standard for tactical operational diving equipment.

115. The only prototype of the suit is in the author's possession.

116. After the war he was charged with performing medical experiments on inmates of the Dachau concentration camp and was sentenced to 20 years in prison. See: Maser, Werner: *Nürnberg – Tribunal der Sieger*. Dusseldorf 1977.

117. At the end of the war all of the design drawings and documents relating to the automatically-controlled mixed gas breathing device invented by Hermann Tietze were seized from the Dräger factory by the British and taken away. Because of the Potsdam Agreement, it was years after the war before Tietze could resume his work and secure it through patents, for example US 3068864 of 23/03/1959.

118. Little remains of the military installations in the harbor, as they were demolished by the British occupation forces after the war. One of the large hangars was disassembled and used in the construction of the Ostseehalle in Kiel. The only remnants of the former military presence are the present-day Naval Supply School (MVS) for 2,000 men of the *Bundeswehr*, the row houses which once housed members of the *Wehrmacht*, and the harbor and concrete surfaces of the Königshafen, the latter now used as a parking lot. In the MVS today, members of the navy receive training in logistics, staff duties and marine first-aid.

119. Wandel's service in Training Detachment 700 ended on 1 February; from then until the end of the war he served as a doctor in the Cottbus refugee camp.

120. Toward the end of the war the organization of the MEK operational groups could no longer be maintained, and individual, more or less independent groups were formed to operate regionally. Among them were *Leutnant* Alfred Keller's "Combat Diver Group East", "Battle Unit Leather Stocking" under *Korvettenkapitän* Hans Bartels, "Battle Unit Panther" under *Kapitänleutnant* Uhde, and "Battle Group Puma" under *Oberleutnant z.S.* Erich Dörpinghaus.

121. Medical log of the medical officer attached to Small Battle Unit Headquarters from 01/01/1944 to 30/11/1944, maintained by Marinestabsarzt Dr. Richert. Bundesarchiv-Militärarchiv RM 103/10.

122. Wandel, Armin: Medical log of the medical officer attached to Training Detachment 700 from 26/02/1944 to 12/04/1944. Wandel estate (Archiv Nöldeke).

123. Wandel, Armin: Medical log of the unit medical officer, ibid.

124. *SS-Hauptsturmführer* Dr. Wetz, IV-b in Skorzeny's operations staff in RSHA Amt VI-S, was responsible for the recruiting and training of medical personnel within the commando units and Amt VI-S. Wetz also developed medical equipment for use in special operations.

125. At the urging of zoologist Harold Jefferson Coolidge, in March 1942 the American armed forces (Naval Research Laboratory) began conducting experiments with chemical shark repellents (copper acetate).

126. Wurzian, Alfred von: *Die Teufelsschwimmer*, ibid.

127. Wurzian, Alfred von: *Die Teufelsschwimmer*, ibid.

128. Sowa later changed his decision and swam after his two comrades. He was not seen again, however, and his fate is not known. This means that five of the six combat divers returned from the first operation.

129. In November the Italian Gamma divers attacked Livorno harbor, but the effort was a failure. See: *Menschen gegen Panzerstahl. Ein britischer Abwehroffizier berichtet über seinen Kampf gegen die geheime Waffe im Mittelmeerkrieg*. 5 parts in: *Norddeutsche Zeitung*, Hanover, 14/01/1950 – 28/01/1950.

130. Wandel, Armin: Appendix to the detachment commander's war diary, ibid.

131. Not the same man as *Oberfähnrich* (MA) Wirth, who was later also stationed in Valdagno. Wirth is mentioned in Manfred Lau's book *Schiffsterben vor Algier* and who was assigned to a mission against the bridge at Remagen with two SLC torpedo vehicles.

132. Wandel, Armin: Appendix to the detachment commander's war diary, ibid.

133. Nöldeke, Hartmut and Hartmann, Volker: *Der Sanitätsdienst in der deutschen U-Boot-Waffe und bei den Kleinkampfverbänden. Geschichte der deutschen U-Boot-Medizin*. Hamburg, 1996, p. 197.

134. Prof. Dr. E. Holzlöhner of the University of Kiel acquired some of his knowledge from hypothermia experiments on prisoners at the Dachau concentration camp. He carried out experiments on cooling of the human body in the cold waters of the North Sea on behalf of the air force and navy, aware that his unwilling subjects might lose their lives in the process. He avoided judgment by the Nuremberg Tribunal by committing suicide. See Prahl, Hans-Werner (publisher): *Uni-Formierung des Geistes. Universität Kiel im Nationalsozialismus*. Kiel 1995.

135. Despite all his risky special operations, Hummel survived the war uninjured. It was an irony of fate and not devoid of a certain element of tragedy that he later suffered physical damage from an unusual "delayed side effect": despite the heart attack he had suffered in 1960, Friedrich Hummel swam regularly well into old age, covering several kilometers in Flensburg Fiord to stay in shape. While vacationing in Spain, he was run down by a speedboat while swimming and sustained serious injuries. The boat operator had simply failed to see him... Hummel's iron will and hard training enabled him to largely regain his mobility.

136. Hummel, Friedrich: *Comments on the description of the operation against the Nijmegen bridges in the book by Waldron and Gleeson.* Typewritten ca. 1950. Archiv Jung.

137. Wandel, Armin: Appendix to the detachment commander's war diary, ibid.

138. *Die Verwegensten.* In *Berlin Illustrierte Zeitung,* Berlin, No. 48 of 30 November 1944, cover page.

139. Between the sea bottom and the water's surface. In *Neues Wiener Tagblatt,* No. 341 of 24/12/1944.

140. Wurzian, Alfred von: *Die Teufelsschwimmer,* ibid.

141. After leaping overboard, Wurzian spent several hours alone in the Adriatic until a torpedo boat finally returned and picked him up.

142. These headquarters were completely disbanded on 30 November 1944 following the transfer of Assault Boat Training Detachments 600, 601 and 602 and Sea Commando Training Detachments 700, 701 (Venice/Alga) and 704 (Valdagno) from Italy to the "White Belt" (List on Sylt). They were absorbed by the Small Battle Unit Headquarters Italy, which was only responsible for the small battle unit flotillas deployed in Italy.

143. Niehoff, Hermann: *So fiel Breslau, Teil V: Ursula sprengte die Brücke.* In: *Welt am Sonntag,* Hamburg, No. 7 of 12 February 1956, p. 9. "Operation Winnetou" was also called "Operation Lucie".

144. Not to be confused with the Knight's Cross wearer of the same name, *Leutnant* (V) Alfred Vetter, who was also a member of the small battle force. From a German fairy tale, "Rübezahl" was a mountain dwarf who was lord of the underworld.

145. A short time later the second group, together with the German unit it had joined when it left the water inside the bridgehead, was captured by the Soviets.

146. Bracke, Gerhard: *Die Einzelkämpfer der Kriegsmarine. Einmanntorpedo- und Sprengbootfahrer im Einsatz.* Stuttgart 1981.

147. In mid-1944 the *Abwehr*'s "*Brandenburg* Division" was reorganized into the "*Brandenburg* Panzer-Grenadier Division" and on 13 September 1944 was integrated into the *Panzer-Korps "Großdeutschland".* In the course of this process every *Brandenburger* was given the choice of remaining with the unit or changing over to the SS commando units under Otto Skorzeny. Skorzeny spoke of 1,800 men who went over to the SS, forming the SS Commando Units Southeast, East, Southwest and Northwest. Most, however, retained their *Wehrmacht* status and rank and were not automatically transformed into SS personnel.

148. Skorzeny, Otto: *Meine Kommandounternehmen,* Wiesbaden, ibid. p. 177. It is not clear if Hummel was already working for Skorzeny prior to autumn 1944, as for example in the SS commando operation against the Danish resistance in January 1944, with which his name has been associated. See Infield, Glenn B.: *Skorzeny: Hitler's Commando.* New York 1981, pp. 50-53.

149. This codename was given by Otto Skorzeny in his book *Meine Kommandounternehmen,* Wiesbaden, p. 177. From September 1944 until the end of the war Hummel, as a member of the SS-RSHA Amt Mil Reg. Kurfürst, was director of the SS Commando Force's Control Center West (formerly the *Abwehr II*'s control center Frontline Intelligence II West), a position equivalent to a regimental commander in the *Wehrmacht.* Hummel later assisted in the writing of a biographical book about Skorzeny and his commando operations. See Foley, Charles: *Kommando Sonderauftrag,* Munich/Wels 1960, p. 10.

150. Skorzeny, Otto: *Wir kämpften – wir verloren.* Siegburg-Niederpleis, ibid. p. 57 and subsequent.

151. See Kern, Erich: *Die letzte Schlacht. Ungarn 1944-45.* Göttingen 1960.

152. The *Kriegsmarine* also had its eye on the Suez Canal as a potential target. The attack was to be made by a miniature submarine, however the problem of transporting the sub to the canal could not be resolved.

153. Skorzeny, Otto: Wir kämpften – wir verloren. Siegburg-Niederpleis, ibid. p. 196.

154. The operation could not be carried out, however. The members of the "Puma" Group were subsequently transferred to the Main River. Oblt.z.S. Dörpinghaus was killed by artillery fire during a mission against the Aschaffenburg locks.

155. From 25 March to 6 April the CDLs illuminated the five pontoon bridges over the Rhine throughout the night to spot divers or floating mines moving downstream. In this way three more German combat divers were captured and numerous drift mines were detonated with small arms fire before they could reach the pontoon bridges.

156. Lauer, Walter E.: *Battle Babies*, Baton Rouge, LA, 1951, p. 214.

157. Friedrich Hummel carried out the operational direction and coordination of the RSHA's combat diver units in personal union with his permanent position of commander of the SS Commando Force's western control center.

SOURCES

Books

Abshagen, Karl Heinz: Canaris. Patriot und Weltbürger. Stuttgart 1949.

Ärztliches Kriegstagebuch des Verbandsarztes beim Kommando der K-Verbände vom 01.01.1944 bis 30.11.1944, geführt vom Marinestabsarzt Dr. Richert. Bundesarchiv-Militärarchiv RM 103/10.

Bagnasco, Erminio, und Spertini, Marco: I mezzi d'assalto X MAS, 1940-1945. Parma 1991.

Banach, Jens: Heydrichs Elite. Das Führungskorps der Sicherheitspolizei und des SD 1936-1945. Paderborn 1998.

Bartz, Karl: Die Tragödie der deutschen Abwehr. Salzburg 1955.

Baum, Walter, und Weichold, Eberhard: Der Krieg der "Achsenmächte" im Mittelmeer-Raum. Göttingen 1973.

Bekker, Cajus [d.i. Hans-Dieter Berenbrok]: Einzelkämpfer auf See. Die deutschen Torpedoreiter, Froschmänner und Sprengbootpiloten im Zweiten Weltkrieg. Herford 1978.

—: Wie unsere Froschmänner es "machten". In: Lies mit. Nummer 13, Juni 1956.

Bergann, Hans-Joachim: Der Produzent. In: tauchen, Hamburg, Heft 7/88, S. 38-39.

Berndt, Helmut: Neue Winkelriede. Die Einmann-Torpedofahrer. In: Das Reich, 10.09.1944.

Bertrand, Michel: Commandos de la mer. 1985.

Borghese, Junio Valerio: Teufel der Tiefe. Boppard a. Rhein 1961.

—: Junio Valerio Borghese e la Xa Flottiglia Mas dall'8 settembre 1943 al aprile 1945. Milano 1996.

Bracke, Gerhard: Die Einzelkämpfer der Kriegsmarine. Einmanntorpedo- und Sprengbootfahrer im Einsatz. Stuttgart 1981.

Bradner, Hugh: Sharks and Shark Repellents. In: Skin Diver, Los Angeles, April 1953, S. 5.

Brammer, Uwe: Spionageabwehr und Geheimer Meldedienst. Die Abwehrstelle im Wehrkreis X Hamburg 1935-1945. Freiburg i.Br. 1989.

Breyer, Siegfried, und Koop, Gerhard: Die Deutsche Kriegsmarine 1935-1945. Band 3: Marine-Kleinkampfverbände u.a., Friedberg 1987.

Brockdorff, Werner: Geheimkommandos des Zweiten Weltkrieges. München-Wels 1968.

Brüne, Lothar, und Weiler, Jakob: Remagen im März 1945. Eine Dokumentation der Schlussphase des Zweiten Weltkriegs. Remagen 1993.

Buchheit, Gert: Der deutsche Geheimdienst. Geschichte der militärischen Abwehr. München 1966.

Buchheim, Hans u.a: Anatomie des SS-Staates. Gutachten des Instituts für Zeitgeschichte. Olten 1965.

Bundesarchiv: Diverses Archivmaterial zu beteiligten Personen.

Burdick, Charles B.: Germany's Military Strategy and Spain in World War II. Syracuse, NY 1968.

Cafiero, Gaetano Nini: Luigi Ferraro. Un Italiano. Formello (Rm) 2000.

Camarasa, Jorge: ODESSA del Sur. La Argentina como refugio de Nazis y criminales de guerra. Buenos Aires 1995.

Charisius, Albrecht, und Moritz, Erhard: Zur Fusion des OKW-Amtes Ausland/Abwehr mit dem Sicherheitsdienst (SD) 1944. In: Militärgeschichte, 16. Jg. (1977), S. 44-57.

Dal Lago, Maurizio: Valdagno 1943-1945. Vicenza 1992.

—: Valdagno 3 luglio 1944. I sette Martiri. Valdagno 2002.

Dal Lago, Maurizio, und Rasia, Franco: Valdagno marzo-giugno 1944 - Dallo sciopero generale all'eccidio di Borga. Valdagno 2004.

Danner, Herwig: Kriegsfischkutter: KFK. Hamburg 2001.

Davis, Robert H.: Deep Diving and Submarine Operations. London 1955.

Demmin, August: Die Kriegswaffen in ihren geschichtlichen Entwicklungen von den ältesten Zeiten bis auf die Gegenwart. Enzyklopädie der Waffenkunde. Wiesbaden 1895/1896.

Derjabin, A.: Osthilfsfreiwillige in Wehrmacht, Polizei, SS, 1939-1945. Moskau o.D.

Detwiler, Donald S.: Hitler, Franco und Gibraltar. Die Frage des spanischen Eintritts in den Zweiten Weltkrieg. Wiesbaden 1962.

Dönitz, Karl: Zehn Jahre und zwanzig Tage. Bonn 1958.

Dörr, Manfred: Die Ritterkreuzträger der Überwasserstreitkräfte der Kriegsmarine. Osnabrück 1995/1996.

Donald, Kenneth: Oxygen and the Diver. Worcester 1992.

Drägerwerk Lübeck (Hrsg.): Drägertauchgeräte schlauchlos und mit Schlauch. Katalog T, 6. deutsche Ausgabe, Lübeck, Februar 1946.

Dreger, Thomas: Geschützter Lebensabend für einen NS-Verbrecher - Otto Skorzeny. tageszeitung taz, Berlin, 12.12.1991, S. 10.

Drobjasko, Sergey, und Karaschuk, A.: Ostlegionen und Kosakeneinheiten in der Wehrmacht 1941-45. Moskau 1998.

Eberl, Erwin: Wehrmachtssport im Zweiten Weltkrieg. In: Deutsches Soldatenjahrbuch 1982. 30. Deutscher Soldatenkalender. München 1982, S. 214-225.

Fellgiebel, Walther-Peer: Die Träger des Ritterkreuzes des Eisernen Kreuzes 1939-1945. Komplettausgabe. Friedberg/Hessen 1993.

Fock, Harald: Marine-Kleinkampfmittel. Bemannte Torpedos, Klein-U-Boote, Klein-Schnellboote, Sprengboote Gestern-heute-morgen. Hamburg 1996.

Foley, Charles: Kommando Sonderauftrag. Tatsachenbericht über Einsätze Otto Skorzenys sowie westlicher Sondereinheiten während des Zweiten Weltkrieges und ihre Folgerungen. München/Wels 1960.

Girelli, Elio: Il palombaro del Pasubio. Venezia 1987.

Grabatsch, Martin: Torpedoreiter, Sturmschwimmer und Sprengbootfahrer. Eine Geheimwaffe im Zweiten Weltkrieg. Wels 1979.

Hagen, Walter: Die geheime Front. Organisation, Personen und Aktionen des deutschen Geheimdienstes. Stuttgart 1950.

Hartmann, V. Pervitin - Vom Gebrauch und Mißbrauch einer Droge in der Kriegsmarine. In: Wehrmedizinische Monatsschrift, 38 (1994), S. 137-142.

Hass, Hans: Menschen und Haie. Zürich 1949.

Haupt, Werner: Deutsche Spezialdivisionen 1935-1945. Wölfersheim-Berstadt 1995.

Haux, Gerhard: Tauchertechnik. Heidelberg 1969/1970.

Hechler, Ken: The Bridge at Remagen. New York 1998.

Heinsius, E.: Zur Geschichte der sinnesmedizinischen Forschungsabteilung der Kriegsmarine in den Jahren 1933-1945. In: Wehrmedizinische Monatsschrift, Bonn, 17 (1973), S. 115-117.

Herrmann, Gustav: Die "Einjährigen". In: Das deutsche Soldatenjahrbuch. München 1977, S. 66-76.

Heye, Hellmuth: Marine-Kleinkampfmittel. In: Wehrkunde, München 1959, S. 413-421.

Hummel, Friedrich: Ritterkreuzträger der Abwehr. In: Das Ritterkreuz. Mitteilungsblatt der Ordensgemeinschaft der Ritterkreuzträger. Wiesbaden, Nr. 2, Juni 1975, S. 13.

—: Stellungnahme zu der Schilderung des Einsatzes gegen die Brücken von Nijmegen im Buch von Waldron und Gleeson. Maschinenschriftliches Manuskript, ca. 1950. Archiv Jung.

Höhne, Heinz: Canaris. Patriot im Zwielicht. München 1979.

—: Der Krieg im Dunkeln. Macht und Einfluss des deutschen Geheimdienstes. München 1985.

Hoff, E.C.: A Bibliographical Sourcebook of Compressed Air, Diving and Submarine Medicine. Navmed 1191. Bureau of Medicine and Surgery. Navy Department. Washington D.C. 1948/1954/1966.

Infield, Glenn B.: Skorzeny: Hitlers Commando. New York 1981.

Innenministerium des Landes Schleswig-Holstein: Personalakte des Kriminalbeamten i.R. Friedrich Hummel. In: Landesarchiv Schleswig, Signatur 621-301.

Jung, Michael: Hans Hass. Ein Leben lang auf Expedition. Ein Porträt. Stuttgart 1994.

—: Das Handbuch zur Tauchgeschichte. Stuttgart 1999.

—: Friedrich Hummel. Topagent, Kampfschwimmer, Pionier (in Vorbereitung).

Kahn, David: Hitler's spies: German military intelligence in World War II. London 1978.

Kaltenegger, Roland: Operationszone "adriatisches Küstenland". Der Kampf um Triest, Istrien und Fiume 1944/45. Stuttgart 1993.

Kampfschwimmerkompanie Eckernförde (Hrsg.): 10 Jahre Kampfschwimmerkompanie. Festschrift zum 10. Jubiläum 1974.

Kapitän Thie: Mit Hans Hass im Ägäischen Meer. Der Kapitän des Expeditionsschiffes erzählt. Berlin/Dahlem 1953.

Keller, Alfred: Leserbrief zu "Ein Schrecken der Russen". In: Welt am Sonntag, Hamburg, Nr. 8 vom 19. Februar 1956, Seite 9.

Kemp, Paul: Bemannte Torpedos und Klein-U-Boote. Stuttgart 1999.

Kern, Erich: Die letzte Schlacht. Ungarn 1944-1945. Göttingen 1960.

Klein, Herbert: Große Leidenschaft: Duschen. In: Der Spiegel, Hamburg, Nr. 13 vom 26.03.1949, S. 13.

—: Es fehlt noch die Goldmedaille. In: Der Spiegel, Hamburg, Nr. 26 vom 25.06.1952. Titelseite, Rückseite und S. 23-26.

—: Ich war ein deutscher Kampfschwimmer. In: Münchner Illustrierte, München, 02.06.1956, S. 8-9.

Knirim, Konrad: Militäruhren. 150 Jahre Zeitmessung beim deutschen Militär. Bottrop 2002.

Kriegsheim, Herbert: Getarnt, Getäuscht und doch Getreu. Die geheimnisvollen "Brandenburger". Berlin 1958.

Kriegstagebuch E-Stab Haun bzw. K-Stab Süd (Admiral Adria) vom 20.09.1944 bis 15.10.1944, geführt von KK Haun. Bundesarchiv-Militärarchiv RM 103/1.

Kugler, Randolf: Die Küstenjäger-Abteilung Brandenburg. In: Schiff und Zeit, Nr. 3, 1978, S. 49 ff.

Kurowski, Franz: Deutsche Kommandotrupps 1939-1945. "Brandenburger" und Abwehr im weltweiten Einsatz. 2 Bände. Stuttgart 2000/2003.

Laak, Ulrich van: Nachruf auf Flottenarzt a.D. Dr. Armin Wandel. In: Wehrmedizinische Monatsschrift, Bonn, Heft 4/1994, S. 132.

Lau, Manfred: Schiffssterben vor Algier. Kampfschwimmer, Torpedoreiter und Marine-Einsatzkommandos im Mittelmeer 1942-1945. Stuttgart 2001.

Lauer, Walter E.: Battle Babies: The Story of the 99th Infantry Division in World War II. Baton Rouge, LA 1951.

Lenz, Siegfried: Der Mann im Strom. München 1995.

Lenzi, Franco: Angelo Belloni: una vita improntata a fantasia, estro e molto talento. In: Bollettino d'Archivio dell'Ufficio Storico della Marina Militare, dicembre 1988.

Lettnin, Heinz K.J.: Tauchen mit Mischgas. Theorie, Technik, Anwendung. Berlin 1994.

Leverkuehn, Paul: Der geheime Nachrichtendienst der deutschen Wehrmacht im Kriege. Frankfurt am Main 1957.

Linck, Stephan: Der Ordnung verpflichtet: Deutsche Polizei 1933-1945. Der Fall Flensburg. Paderborn 2000.

—: Zur Personalpolitik der britischen Besatzungsmacht gegenüber der deutschen Kriminalpolizei nach 1945. In: Fürmetz, Gerhard u.a. (Hrsg.): Nachkriegspolizei. Sicherheit und Ordnung in Ost- und Westdeutschland 1945-1949. Hamburg 2001, S. 105-128.

Lohmann, Walter, und Hildebrand, Hans H.: Die deutsche Kriegsmarine 1939-1945. Gliederung, Einsatz, Stellenbesetzung. Bad Nauheim 1956-1964.

Lucas, James: Kommando: German Special Forces of World War Two. London 1985.

Mader, Julius: Jagd nach dem Narbengesicht. Ein Dokumentarbericht über Hitlers SS-Geheimdienstchef Otto Skorzeny. Berlin-Ost 1962.

Maser, Werner: Nürnberg - Tribunal der Sieger. Düsseldorf 1977.

Mauntz, v.: Gesundheitliche Gefahren des Taucherdienstes und Tauchererkrankungen. Der Deutsche Militärarzt 3 (1937), S. 452-456.

Meding, Holger M.: Flucht vor Nürnberg Deutsche und österreichische Einwanderung in Argentinien 1945-1955. Köln 1992.

Mehner, Kurt: Die Waffen-SS und Polizei 1939-45. Norderstedt 1995. Darin: Aufstellungbefehl für die SS-Jagdverbände, 4. Okt. 1944, Tgb.Nr. 3473/44.

Melton, Keith H.: OSS Special Weapons and Equipment: Spy Devices of World War II. New York 1991.

Munoz, Antonio J.: Forgotten Legions. Obsure Combat Formations of the Waffen-SS. Boulder/ Colorado 1991.

—: Forgotten Legions Companion Book. Additional data for the classic study. New York ca. 2000.

Nachwuchsabteilung des Oberkommandos der Kriegsmarine (Hrsg.): Marinekampfschwimmer. Faltblatt, November 1944.

Niehoff, Hermann: So fiel Breslau. Teil V: Ursula sprengte die Brücke. In: Welt am Sonntag, Hamburg. Nr. 7 vom 12. Februar 1956, Seite 9.

Negretti, Giampiero: Panerei Historia. In der Tiefe des Meeres. Milano 1999.

—: Taucheruhren der Officine Panerei. Milano 1997.

Nöldeke, Hartmut, und Hartmann, Volker: Der Sanitätsdienst in der deutschen U-Boot-Waffe und bei den Kleinkampfverbänden. Geschichte der deutschen U-Boot-Medizin. Hamburg 1996.

Oberkommando der Kriegsmarine: Dienstanweisung für Taucher. Berlin 1939.

Ochwadt, Curd: Das Steinhuder Meer. Hannover 1967.

Ouvaroff, Serge: Torpilles Humaines. Paris 1951.

Petersson, Ingo: Ein sonderlicher Haufen. Die Saga vom Sturmbataillon 500. Neckargemünd 1959.

Piekalkiewicz, Janusz: Spione, Agenten, Soldaten. Geheime Kommandos im Zweiten Weltkrieg. München 1988.

Pöschel, Günther: Froschmänner, Torpedoreiter, Zwerg-U-Boote. Berlin 1961.

Pomorin, Jürgen, u.a.: Blutige Spuren - Der zweite Aufstieg der SS. Dortmund 1980.

—: Geheime Kanäle - Der Nazi-Mafia auf der Spur. Dortmund 1982.

Prahl, Hans-Werner (Hrsg): Uni-Formierung des Geistes. Universität Kiel im Nationalsozialismus. Kiel 1995.

Probst, Wilhelm: Kampfschwimmer der Bundesmarine. Innenansichten einer Elitetruppe. Stuttgart 2001.

Querg, Thorsten J.: Spionage und Terror: Das Amt VI des Reichssicherheitshauptamtes 1939-1945. Berlin 1997.

Ricciotti, Lazzero: La decima Mas. Milano 1984.

Ryan, Cornelius: Die Brücke von Arnheim. Frankfurt 1975.

Sadkovich, James J.: The Italian Navy in World War II. London 1984.

Saint-Loup: Yachten in geheimer Mission. Segler im Dienste der Abwehr. Bielefeld 1988.

Schellenberg, Walter: Memoiren. Köln 1956.

Schenck, Hans-Joachim: Die Geschichte der K-Flottille 416 (6. Molch). In: MOH-Nachrichten. Krefeld, 4 Teile vom 15.02.1954-15.07.1954.

Schenck, Peter: Kampf um die Ägäis. Die Kriegsmarine in Griechischen Gewässern 1941-1945. Hamburg 2000.

Schenk, Dieter: Die Charlottenburger. Wie Nationalsozialisten das Bundeskriminalamt aufbauten. In: tageszeitung taz, Berlin, 4./5. März 2000.

—: Auf dem rechten Auge blind - die braunen Wurzeln des BKA. Köln 2001.

Scheurig, Bodo: Alfred Jodl. Gehorsam und Verhängnis. Schnellbach 1999.

Schneider, Hans-Ulrich (Hrsg.): Das OKW muss schweigen. In: Freie Presse. Deutsche Wochenzeitung am La Plata. Buenos Aires. 10 Teile vom 08.10.1951-23.10.1951.

Schofield, William, und Carisella, P.J.: Frogmen: First Battles. Boston 1987.

Schulze-Kossens, Richard: Militärischer Führernachwuchs der Waffen-SS. Die Junkerschulen. Osnabrück 1982.

Seemen, Gerhard von: Die Ritterkreuzträger 1939-1945. Friedberg/Hessen 1976.

Skorzeny, Otto: Geheimkommando Skorzeny. Hamburg 1950.

—: Der gefährlichste Mann der Welt. Meine Memoiren. 11 Teile. In: Quick, Illustrierte für Deutschland, Heft 14-24, 1950.

—: Lebe gefährlich. Skorzenys Erinnerungen, Band 1. Siegburg-Niederpleis 1962.

—: Wir kämpften - wir verloren. Skorzenys Erinnerungen, Band 2. Siegburg-Niederpleis 1962.

—: Meine Kommandounternehmen. Krieg ohne Fronten. Wiesbaden 1976.

—: SS-Jagdverbände. In: Der Freiwillige, Pulach, Heft 7/8 1992, S. 24.

Staatsanwaltschaft am Kieler Landgericht: Ermittlungsverfahren zum Partisaneneinsatz in Borga und in der Strafsache Rockstroh. Aktenzeichen-Nummer - 2 JS 173/65 -. Landesarchiv Schleswig Abt. 352 Kiel Nr. 1158.

Stelzner, Hermann: Tauchertechnik. Lübeck 1943.

Tarrant, V.E.: Das letzte Jahr der deutschen Kriegsmarine: Mai 1944-Mai 1945. Wölfersheim 1996.

Tessin, Georg: Verbände und Truppen der deutschen Wehrmacht und Waffen-SS im Zweiten Weltkrieg 1939-1945. Osnabrück 1965-1980.

Thomer, Egbert [d.i. Jan Mayen]: Sprung an die Küste: amphibische Streitkräfte, Geschichte und Gegenwart. Oldenburg 1963.

Tietze, Hermann: Halboffenes Atemschutzgerät mit Helium-Sauerstoff-Gemisch für Versuche im Druckkessel. In: Dräger-Hefte (1958) 232, S. 5023-5027.

Vietinghoff-Scheel, Heinrich von: La Fine della Guerra in Italia (Recoaro, ottobre 1944 - aprile 1945). Valdagno 1997.

Vigano, Marino: Guerra segretta sotta i Mare. Eugenio Wolk e i "Gamma" della Decima Mas (1942-1945). In: Storia del XX Secolo, Casteggio (PV), No. 6-8, ottobre - dicembre 1995.

Voigt, Horst: Die "verlornen Haufen". Sondertruppen zur Frontbewährung im 2. Weltkrieg. 18 Teile, In: Deutsches Soldatenjahrbuch. Deutscher Soldatenkalender. 1980-1998. München.

Wagner, Patrick: Volksgemeinschaft ohne Verbrecher: Konzeption und Praxis der Kriminalpolizei in der Zeit der Weimarer Republik und des Nationalsozialismus. Hamburg 1996.

—: Hitlers Kriminalisten. Die deutsche Kriminalpolizei und der Nationalsozialismus. München 2002.

Waldron, Tom J., und Gleeson, James: The Frogmen. The story of the wartime underwater Operators. London 1950.

Wandel, Armin: Die Panik beim Schiffbruch - ein medizinisches und Führungsproblem. In: Truppenpraxis, 12/1969, S. 23-29.

—: Ärztliches Kriegstagebuch des Abteilungsarztes bei der Marine-Einsatz-Abteilung vom 26.02.1944 bis 12.04.1944. Nachlass Wandel (Archiv Nöldeke).

—: Ärztliches Kriegstagebuch des Arztes beim E.u.A.Stab Süd vom 03.05.1944 bis 18.05.1944. Nachlass Wandel (Archiv Nöldeke).

—: Kriegstagebuch des Kommandochefs des Marine-Lehrkommandos 700 vom 21.06.1944 bis 30.09.1944 nebst Anlagen. Nachlass Wandel (Archiv Nöldeke).

—: Schreiben an den Admiralstabsarzt a.D. Dr. med. Emil Greul vom 29.10.1990. Nachlass Greul (Archiv Nöldeke).

—: Stirb und Werde. Dokumente einer schlesischen Familientragödie. Lahr/ Schwarzwald, Selbstverlag, 1990. Nachlass Wandel (Archiv Nöldeke).

Warren, C.E.T., und Benson, James: und über uns die Wogen. Jugenheim 1960.

Welham, Michael: Kampfschwimmer. Geschichte, Ausrüstung, Einsätze. Stuttgart 1996.

Wighton, Charles, und Peis, Günter: Hitler's Spies and Saboteurs. New York 1958.

Wildt, Michael: Generation des Unbedingten. Das Führungskorps des Reichssicherheitshauptamtes. Hamburg 2002.

Witzel, Dietrich F.: Kommandoverbände der Abwehr II im Zweiten Weltkrieg. In: Militärgeschichtliches Forschungsamt (HRSG.): Militärgeschichtliches Beiheft zur Europäischen Wehrkunde. Heft 5, Oktober 1990.

Wurzian, Alfred von: Wunder der Meerestiefe. In: Allgemeine Thüringische Landeszeitung Deutschland, 10.02.1943.

—: Auf Korallen- und Haifischjagd in der Aegäis. In: Thüringer Gauzeitung, Arnstadt, 22.03.1943.

—: Elf Minuten ohne Luft. In: Beilage zum Hamburger Echo, 31.03.1949, S. 5.

—: Unterwasserjagd auf Haie. In: 1. Beilage zum Hamburger Echo, 19.02.1949, S. 5.

—: Die Teufelsschwimmer. 2 Teile in: Hamburger Abendblatt, Beilage, 1953, BL 25/40.

—: Autobiografische Aufzeichnungen zu dem Zeitraum Oktober 1942 - April 1943. Abgefasst in den Jahren 1968-1970. Archiv Jung.

—: Autobiografische Erinnerungen zu dem Zeitraum 1942-1945 mit Reinhard Penninger auf Tonbändern. Archiv Jung.

—: Briefwechsel mit Hans Hass aus den Jahren 1942-1950. Archiv Jung.

Articles

Der Einmann-Torpedo von Walter Gerhold. In: Berliner Illustrierte Zeitung, Berlin, Nr. 31 vom 03. August 1944, Titelseite.

Die Verwegensten - Deutsche Kampfschwimmer sprengen die Brücke von Nijmegen. In: Berliner Illustrierte Zeitung, Berlin, Nr. 48 vom 30. November 1944, Titelseite und S. 566-567 und Münchner Illustrierte Presse, Nr. 48 vom 30. November 1944. Titelseite und S. 566-567.

Friedrich Hummel verabschiedet. In: Flensburger Tageblatt, 31.03.1970.

German attempt to Blow up Bridges. In: The Times, London, 6 October 1944, p. 4 column b.

In der Morgendämmerung kehren sie heim. Sprengboote und Einmann-Torpedos. In: Berliner Illustrierte Zeitung, Berlin, Nr. 38 vom 21. September 1944, Titelseite und S. 446.

Italiens Geheimwaffe - zum erstenmal im Bild gezeigt. Zweimann-Torpedos. In: Berliner Illustrierte Zeitung. Berlin, Nr. 25 vom 24. Juni 1943, S. 292.

Menschen gegen Panzerstahl. Ein britischer Abwehroffizier berichtet über seinen Kampf gegen die geheime Waffe im Mittelmeerkrieg. 5 Teile in: Norddeutsche Zeitung, Hannover, 14.01.1950-28.01.1950.

Neues Kampfmittel: Einmanntorpedo. Ein neuer Einzelkämpfertyp. In: Wiener Neueste Nachrichten. Wien, den 18. Juli 1944. Nr. 7545, Nachtausgabe. S. 1.

Neues Kampfmittel: Sprengboote. In: Völkischer Beobachter. Berliner Ausgabe, 16.09.1944.

The Frogmen: A german idea in Warfare. In: Picture Post. London, Vol. 26. No. 4, vom 27. Januar 1945, S. 20-21.

Zwischen Meeresgrund und Wasserspiegel. In: Neues Wiener Tagblatt, Nr. 341 vom 24.12.1944 und Potsdamer Tageszeitung vom 02.02.1945 und Deutsche Zeitung in Norwegen, Oslo, vom 12.02.1945 und Der Führer, Karlsruhe, vom 07.02.1945 und Mitteldeutsche National-Zeitung, Halle, 23.02.1945.

Photos

Archiv Wurzian: Seite 18, 36, 37, 39, 40 l., 51, 54, 57, 70, 78, 79, 80, 81, 82, 85, 91, 94, 110, 111, 112 u., 134.

Archiv Jung: Seite 11, 13, 30, 38, 40 r., 53, 103, 105, 106, 118, 119 l.

Nachlass Wandel (Archiv Nöldeke): Seite 58, 62, 69, 71, 73, 84, 88, 104, 107, 112 o.

Familie Hummel: Seite 115, 119 r.

Heinz-Werner Sondermann: Seite 135.

Luigi Ferraro: Seite 76.

Friedensmuseum Brücke von Remagen e.V.: Seite 129.

Knirim, Konrad: Militäruhren. 150 Jahre Zeitmessung beim deutschen Militär. Bottrop 2002: Seite 42.